THE
NECESSITY OF ART

BY

A. CLUTTON BROCK, PERCY DEARMER,
A. S. DUNCAN-JONES, J. MIDDLETON MURRY,
A. W. POLLARD, AND MALCOLM SPENCER

WIPF & STOCK · Eugene, Oregon

Wipf and Stock Publishers
199 W 8th Ave, Suite 3
Eugene, OR 97401

The Necessity of Art
By Clutton Brock, Arthur and Dearmer, Percy
ISBN 13: 978-1-5326-7096-1
Publication date 9/25/2018
Previously published by SCM, 1924

CONTENTS

	PAGE
PREFACE	v

CHAPTER
I. ART AND THE ESCAPE FROM BANALITY . 1
   A. CLUTTON BROCK

II. CHRISTIANITY AND ART 29
   PERCY DEARMER

III. THE ART OF MOVEMENT 75
   A. S. DUNCAN-JONES

IV. THE PURITAN OBJECTION TO ART . . 101
   MALCOLM SPENCER

V. THE ARTIST AND THE SAINT . . . 121
   ALFRED W. POLLARD

VI. LITERATURE AND RELIGION . . . 137
   J. MIDDLETON MURRY

VII. THE DOCTRINE OF VALUES . . . 167
   PERCY DEARMER

NOTE

As this volume is going through the press, there comes the news of the death to-day of Arthur Clutton Brock. The loss to the world of thought is great indeed, for he was almost alone in his combined intensity and breadth of mind. He understood; and he differed from most clever men in having no blind side. Acutely sensitive, unerringly sane, without a touch of sentimentality or of its common harsh inversion, he was building up a coherent philosophy of life, and his philosophy was as large as life. His chapter in this volume is the last contribution to that work which we hoped he would live to finish. It was in his house that our meetings took place; all our contributions were worked out with his help, and had his approval; he was himself to have written the last chapter on the Doctrine of Values —a working philosophy now widely spread by those writings of his, which were often scattered anonymously in the pages of the *Times*,—but he was prevented by illness. The last chapter of this book is therefore an attempt to convey a part of his message; and he saw it in proof during that long illness throughout which his intellect was as acute as ever. The best presentment of that foundation upon which we have all tried to build, is his masterly little outline, *The Ultimate Belief;* and, for our part, we are convinced that in the writing which he has left behind him lies the clue by which the world may escape from its long confusion and come into the light.

January 8th, 1924.

PREFACE

THERE is in the world to-day a conviction of sin about art. People realize more every year that the badness of our architecture, decoration, music, drama, which has been our legacy from the immediate past, is an offence against the highest that is in us; they are discarding both the bleak indifference of our puritan tradition and the decadent hedonism which was a reaction against it: everywhere in all the arts there is improvement—a return to sincerity, simplicity, beauty; and the improvement is due to the growing conviction of the high seriousness of art. We are less tempted to regard the arts because of their delightfulness as a mere pastime; we are discovering that in them we touch the eternal world—that art is in fact religious. The object of art is not to give pleasure, as our fathers assumed, but to express the highest spiritual realities. Art is not only delightful: it is necessary.

But there are still difficulties, and the main obstacle to the complete revival of art is a theoretical one which is due to misunderstandings, especially perhaps at the moment on the part of artists themselves, though the philosophers, historians and theologians of the past must bear the ultimate responsibility. We have endeavoured in this volume to remove the misunderstandings, in the hope that we may be able to do a little towards clearing the way for an authoritative philosophy of æsthetic.

Art, we believe, cannot be understood unless it is

THE NECESSITY OF ART

realized as part of life as a whole, and especially of religion, which is itself an expression of an intense interest in life. The explanation of art cannot be that it is the mere production of beautiful objects in the realm of matter; the dreariness indeed of much current æsthetic life and thought is caused by that blindness to the eternal values which has been inherited from a quantitative and materialistic phase of thought. Recent writers upon æsthetic, including Lord Balfour, Mr Roger Fry, and Mr Clive Bell, have recognized that—if one thinks far enough into the problem, one is brought to the edge of " mysticism." We agree with them; we should only plead for the more homely word, religion, and add that this is no reason for stopping the quest, as at the brink of some perilous chasm; but that we must take the plunge, and then we shall find, not indeed that we understand all that is contained in that great word, but that the waters are bracing and sustaining—that in fact we have in religion a hypothesis which bears us on towards the goal of our quest and enables us to adjust ourselves to all the facts of life.

But, if art and religion are the two chief factors in the adjustment, a good deal of misunderstanding on both sides needs removing. Perhaps one need not press upon the ministers of the Christian religion their failure in the past to realize the fundamental elements of Christ's message to the world: they are already alive to the fact. But the problems involved are too complex to be dismissed in a sentence, and we have devoted a chapter to puritanism, as we have devoted our opening chapter to the problem of the ordinary man who is not a puritan but a, frequently unsuccessful, seeker after happiness. On the other hand, many artists are hampered by the prevalent ignorance of the historic relations between religion and art. There

PREFACE

could be no better spokesman for our finest painters to-day than Sir William Orpen, and he has recently asserted in his introduction to the *Outline of Religion and Art*, which is now appearing, the opposition of Christianity to art from the earliest days, without any suspicion that the facts are the precise opposite to what he has been brought up to believe. He speaks, as it seems, for the great majority of artists, and the misapprehension which he expresses makes us feel that we were justified in giving some space to the historic relations of Christianity and art.

We have adopted the method of a symposium, and have spent many days in conference together. The various chapters are meant to be parts of a connected whole, and in order that they should at the same time bring different points of view to the elucidation of our problems, the symposium method was necessary. The subject of the arts of movement, for instance, is too seldom included in discussions of this sort, because music, with its sisters of the dance and the drama, belongs to a world of special capacities that is apart—unfortunately too far apart at the present day—from what is generally called the art-world. It is also too commonly forgotten that literature is an art, and this subject required special treatment from its own side. Finally, the modesty of artists seemed to require that the delicate comparison between the artist and the saint should be undertaken by an observer from the British Museum. We can only hope that we may help in some small measure both to increase among artists the sense of their high vocation and to further in the world at large, the conviction already widespread, that art is necessary to the spiritual life.

P. D.

New Year's Day 1924.

I
ART AND THE ESCAPE FROM BANALITY

THE NECESSITY OF ART

I

ART AND THE ESCAPE FROM BANALITY

By A. Clutton Brock

We are always lamenting and repenting of our wickedness; but even in that we flatter ourselves. A man would rather confess the sins he has not committed than the sins he has, for he can choose the former but not the latter; and so, when we say that we are desperately wicked, we deceive ourselves. Our real sin is not wickedness but something less dignified and exciting, for which I know no word except the half-French one, Banality. Commonplaceness is clumsy and also less expressive of the exasperation which the French, perhaps, feel more than we do against the commonplace, against sameness where things ought not to be the same. Banality is a word then for sameness where it ought not to be, that is to say in things of the mind. There is a sameness of Nature that does not weary us, innumerable blades of grass, or the sun rising every morning; but human sameness is wearisome because the very virtue of human activities, whether moral, intellectual, or æsthetic, is in differentiation. When men all think alike, they are not thinking at all; when they will alike, they are not willing at all; and common form in art is failure.

We become ourselves by differentiation and we admire a man who is distinct in all that he says and does, feeling that he is more himself than most people are.

THE NECESSITY OF ART

He has character, we say; and this character, this strong difference, pleases us in itself, æsthetically if not morally. Our vitality is heightened by it, as it is lowered by a man who seems undifferentiated in all things, as if he were trying to escape notice by being like other men. This does not mean that we should aim at mere differentiation and try to be unlike everyone else, for that is aiming at a symptom; and those who do it are themselves an undifferentiated herd, alike in their emphasized difference. But it is sillier to aim at sameness than at differentiation for its own sake. To aim at sameness is to aim at what you are to start with, as if you said: "I will go where I am." Sameness is behind us all: the further back we go in the history of living things, the more sameness there is, and it is a mark either of backwardness or of regression: monkeys are more like each other than men, and leading articles than poems. Yet sameness is not only aimed at by the timid; it is also justified by biological theories. We are told that we are herd-animals, not satirically, but as a statement of fact; and there are people who believe that we can be strong and happy and realize the purpose of our being only if we know that we are herd-animals and behave accordingly. To believe this is worse than to do it, for it is a submission of the mind, and of all human hopes, to an imaginary biological necessity; and it is never sincere, for no man believes that he himself is a herd-animal, nor does he like the banality of those who behave like herd-animals. The desire of every man is by some means to escape from this sameness, this banality, even if he does not know how to set about it.

Nor are animals herd-animals because they act alike. All animals of the same kind have a sameness of behaviour, because they are animals and in most things they are

ART AND THE ESCAPE FROM BANALITY

practical, that is, subdued to the business of self-preservation and procreation. Instincts make animals behave alike, and human beings also when they are subject to them. Cats, which are not herd-animals, hunt and lap in the same way and utter the same love-songs. We do not call them banal, because we expect sameness in them; but in ourselves we do not expect it. A man's love-song should be his own, not a caterwauling of the herd or the species, because it is the business of a man's life to rise above the sameness of instinct into that differentiation which is a mark of spiritual activity. We are not interested in the expression of mere instinct, whether erotic or of self-preservation; love becomes interesting to us only when it is differentiated, when it has the individual's character, conscience, sense of beauty, in it; and a love-song should combine the force of instinct with the subtlety of differentiation. If it does not, it is still mere caterwauling.

But, however much we may be wearied by banality in others, it does not seem sinful to us in ourselves. When we are bored with our own sameness, we believe that something outside us is boring us; we do not understand that the wages of banality is boredom, or that a great part of our most disastrous folly, and even wickedness, is the result of that boredom and of the blind effort to escape from it by means of some crude external excitement. Men fall in love where they should not, they turn to drink or drugs or gambling, to escape from their boredom and the banality that causes it. They gather together and lose their identity in mobs, they cheer when war is declared; all because they hope by some violent means to escape from the sameness of their lives, which is really the sameness of their own crude, undifferentiated

THE NECESSITY OF ART

selves. But these violent means increase the ill they are meant to cure. The more men fight or gamble or drink, or surrender themselves to the sexual instinct, the more alike they become. We see this clearly enough when we ourselves are not engaged in any of these mistaken efforts. Race-meeting crowds, gamblers at Monte Carlo, mobs of hostile patriots, such as the Germans in the late war, couples mooning in a lane, or drunkards crooning by themselves, are tiresomely generic to us; and we resent that sameness in them because it seems to rob us of our vitality and life of its meaning, to drag our imaginations back to a common stock of automatic behaviour. I remember watching, before the war, two Germans quarrelling and encouraging their rage against each other because, no doubt, they felt that they were possessed by something great and becoming like Siegfried. But to me, cool and full of English differences, they were generic and even automatic; with each guttural noise and shaking of the fist and paroxysm of the features, they fell back more and more into the unconscious and undifferentiated, became more and more like Tweedledum and Tweedledee; and it seemed strange that there should be such difference between them. Yet they were, no doubt, enjoying the violence of their feelings as an escape from routine; and, if I had been in a rage, I should have enjoyed my own violence and felt that I, too, was possessed by something great.

We all hoped, when the war broke out, that, by that violent, external means, we should escape from our banality, or, as Mr Bottomley said, that life would become real to us at last; and it seemed a cruel practical joke of Nature or Providence, or whatever we believed in, that after the first glow was past, we found ourselves more

ART AND THE ESCAPE FROM BANALITY

banal and unreal than ever, that we repeated formulæ like gramophones and behaved generically like animals; that our theatres were filled with savage or voluptuous dullness, and our churches with bright, breezy irreligion; that we believed any nonsense like primitive man, were possessed by spy and persecution manias, and feared even for one moment to say anything we really meant, lest it should help the enemy. We did not know it then, but fear, the most banal of all passions, was the ultimate cause of our automatisms; for, when men are afraid, they try to escape from the feeling of fear, which, being entirely negative, is entirely disagreeable, by turning it into something positive, namely hatred. Hatred is fear taking the offensive, trying to do something, no matter what; but the automatism of fear remains in its active form; and, as we behave like animals in a panic, so we are still generic when, filled with the bravery of rage, we turn and charge. In fact, the banality of hatred is more exasperating to the observer who does not share it than the banality of fear, because it is active and offensive, and because the victim of it is able actually to enjoy his fear disguised.

And then, when the peace came, we were filled with an obstinate *malaise;* after the war, we had told ourselves, we should reconstruct—everything, but ourselves; we should escape from banality and that generic functioning which danger and patriotism had imposed on us; the very churches had promised themselves that once again they would remember the Sermon on the Mount. But alas! four years of war had imposed habits upon us from which the proclamation of an Armistice did not free us. For the sake of victory, an immediate, practical task, we had become altogether practical, like animals, using

THE NECESSITY OF ART

thought, art, religion and all the virtues, all the human and spiritual part of ourselves so slowly and painfully acquired, for that single, immediate end. Being men, we had, under the compulsion of war, regressed into herd-animals; and now the desire to be men again was in conflict with the herd habit, so that we were sick of ourselves and each other. The wonder is that this nausea, this desire for freedom so blind and so exasperated in its blindness, has not produced a catastrophe. The reason is, no doubt, that we are sick of fighting. But the danger is not yet over; resentment smoulders without having found an object; at any moment it might find one, and unite all discontent in some, probably absurd, purpose.

The war has not cured us of our banality, and the peace has not cured us; but still we long to escape from it. We can never be satisfied with any philosophy or religion which tells us that banal we are and banal we must be. For a century we have been engaged in telling what were believed to be unpleasant truths about ourselves; and we have looked forward to a time when, freed from all illusions, we should be at rest, content with an efficient animality, hoping nothing, fearing nothing, and happily engaged in the struggle for life. We had got the habit of suppressing, even denying, our strongest and most permanent desires, those which in the Middle Ages did express themselves, however wildly, in towering expressions of faith, paradises of stone, music, dancing, painting, drama,—all meaning something, namely the life that men really wished to live, and the universe they wished to believe in. The wish remains, but the means of expressing it are gone; and as Blake says, desire without action breeds pestilence. We made a life we did not wish to live; we conceived a universe

ART AND THE ESCAPE FROM BANALITY

we did not wish to believe in; and the result was dullness, banality, from which we try to escape by violence of feeling, thought, and action. This violence increases but brings no remedy; and now we are, after all our triumphs over the external world, thrown back upon the pressing, practical task of finding some remedy for it and for the dullness which provokes it.

No one can deny that the task is pressing. The efficient, conscious animality at which we have aimed proves to be not efficient because we cannot endure its dullness. There is something in us which refuses its consent to the life we had resolved to live and the universe we had resolved to believe in; and refusal grows stronger, discontent is cumulative. Once before, at least, the same thing has happened. The Greco-Roman world under the Empire grew weary of itself, the life it was living, the universe it believed in. It was, like our own society, highly organized, powerful, impressive. It had a religion, worshipping itself and its own order under the name of the Emperor; it aimed at uniformity in all things and all parts, one bureaucracy regulating everything, one art producing the same statues, monuments, temples and public works everywhere. Compared with the primitive disorder outside its frontiers, it seemed irresistibly strong; and yet, because it could not endure its own dullness, there came a century of purposeless violence, after the Antonines, which destroyed that strength from within. That may happen to us too, is sure to happen, unless we find a remedy for our dullness, a life we can enjoy and a universe we can wish to believe in. The war was but an outburst of the violence which had long been gathering and which took different forms in different countries. In Germany, resentment against other nations; here, resentment between classes, sexes, and races. Germany saved us for the moment from civil war; but our present exhaustion is merely exhaustion; it is not the solution of any problem, and the problem remains to be solved.

But first we need to be aware of its nature, to discover why we are permanently and collectively discontented; and most of us at present do not get beyond the expression, either in words or in actions, of our discontent, the causes of which remain in the unconscious. This expression cannot produce a remedy; it is like the restlessness of a man who turns from side to side in the hope that he will find a position in which he can sleep, and who only increases his sleeplessness by turning.

Further, we are hindered from discovering the cause of our discontent by a whole system of beliefs, often half unconsciously held, which, themselves, are among the causes of our discontent, since they help to produce the banality of our lives. We believe, for instance, that ultimately we are driven, as if we were machines, by our instincts alone; and that these instincts disguise themselves for our consciousness in forms flattering to that consciousness; though why there should be a consciousness at all, which is itself illusion and desires only to be deluded, no one has ever explained. Why, if we are really all sex and the instinct of self-preservation, we should not have the compensations of that crudity and live the simple Freudian life, Freud himself does not tell us. The fact remains, however, that we are not content with this version of ourselves, however much we may try to believe it and to act upon it; and this fact is a fact of our own natures, much more certain and obvious than the version with which we are discontented.

ART AND THE ESCAPE FROM BANALITY

What we desire, finally and permanently, is not to be all alike in the recognition and satisfaction of the same simple instincts; but to attain to ourselves by differentiation; and this desire becomes stronger the more it is denied and suppressed. I am astonished, I confess, at all this talk about the suppressed sexual instinct among people who do not appear to suppress it, since they talk of nothing else. Our whole society, so far from suppressing it, seems to be occupied with expressing it. The " eternal feminine " is the chief theme of our art; and it becomes monotonous, it ceases to be art, because it has no other theme.

No, if we are to talk about suppression at all, let us face the plain fact that what is suppressed in us is not the sexual or any other instinct, but the desire for expression, not the flesh but the spirit. You may dogmatically deny the existence of spirit; but the symptoms of thwarted spiritual expression are everywhere, and with these you have to deal, call them what you will. Take for instance the case of music in England. A German book before the war described England as the Land Without Music. We may reply that we have many concerts, that is to say we hire experts to perform for us; but that is not a musical expression that can satisfy us, any more than the sexual instinct can be satisfied by two actors making passionate but professional love on the stage. If you would see the justice of that German's description, listen to a chorus of English Cockneys,— always a thwarted, shamefaced noise. There is the desire for expression checked by impotence and unconscious inhibitions; and the result is a nasal drone parodying all the emotions it would express if it could and dared. I know no sound or sight more expressive of failure and

THE NECESSITY OF ART

unhappiness; and they would not be able to endure it themselves, if there were not in them a desire for expression so strong that it must find some vent. It is the blasphemy of those who rail against that in which they believe; it is the cry of the dispossessed who cannot recover their rights, because they do not know what they have lost. They wail like lost spirits, and try to console themselves by turning their wail to laughter, not knowing that it might be turned to music.

And this instance of failure of expression is a proof of the importance of expression. For if you have the desire for it without the power, what you express is not what you wish to express but something else; and this something else, because you express it, actually changes that which you wish to express into its own failure. So our Cockneys, when they try to sing, and fail, do come to feel like their own failure and to believe that the reality of their own minds, and of everything else, is a parody of desire. In all things, if we cannot say what we think or feel, we come to think and feel what we say. Nothing in our minds fully exists without expression of some kind; and if the expression, by failure, thwarts the impulse, then the impulse itself deteriorates into the failure.

Another instance of this is our ecclesiastical art, whether of architecture, decoration, or music. There is the impulse towards religious expression in all its forms but, because it fails, it becomes its own failure. You may try to preserve belief in creeds and you may repeat them week by week in church; but if the church in which they are said fails to express anything that any one really feels, then that failure, that impotent insincerity, will, by mere force of association, infect the

ART AND THE ESCAPE FROM BANALITY

very creed which will become a mere form of words as modern Gothic is a mere form of art; and you will feel, even if you do not think, that you go to church to perform a duty as meaningless as the architecture of the church itself. If you doubt this, consider how surely, when a clergyman, from lack of technique or any other cause, says a prayer as if it were a form that no one believed in, you find yourself ceasing to believe in it. He himself, because he cannot express his own impulse to pray in that prayer, expresses something else, probably a silly formalism; and that, associating itself with the prayer, infects your mind also. The reason is because his impulse and your impulse do not fully exist until they are expressed; and, if they are misexpressed, then the impulse through that misexpression changes its very nature. The clergy now constantly lament the spread of unbelief: they do not understand that their task is not merely to preserve belief, which is impossible, for it is not something that can be bottled secure from harm. Belief is never something that exists already in the mind and, remaining there, can be protected from external assault. There is only the impulse to belief, as there are impulses to thought, and these impulses do not fulfil themselves until they are expressed. If they are misexpressed, then they never fulfil themselves but become their own misexpressions. No doubt the writer of a leading article often has the impulse to say something; but, through failure of expression, he says something quite different, namely what other writers of leading articles say. He has failed in differentiation, which is the essence of all expression and has fallen into platitude; it is not he who speaks, but a gramophone, and he becomes the gramophone that has perverted his impulse.

THE NECESSITY OF ART

This gramophone tendency is the danger that besets all highly organized societies. They tend to sacrifice themselves to a machinery which needs more brains and energy than they possess to control it. Samuel Butler's fantasy of the machines that come to life and tyrannize over the human beings who tend them is almost true of us now; and it is not merely actual machines but the very social process that tyrannizes over us. It is not only in factories but in our government, our amusements, our thought, our war, and all our collective activities, that we become more and more like hands, incessantly doing the same little, monotonous job, specialized and regimented by division of labour. But to submit to this is — "Propter vitam vivendi perdere causas." You may sacrifice too much to civilization, as the Romans discovered; you may sacrifice civilization itself, and find that your life is no longer worth living. This you may never say to yourself; but,—if your very mind becomes mechanical, if you are all content to say the same things, which are untrue, and to do the same things, without seeing any reason for doing them,—then in the collective mind there will grow a cumulative disgust which will at last manifest itself in violence and all kinds of unreason, all the more dangerous because the pretexts on which they seize are not the real reasons for their existence, because underlying them there is the desire without action that breeds pestilence; and that desire is for expression, differentiation, the fullness of humanity.

What we need then, if we are to avoid this imminent danger, is, first of all, a certain set of beliefs about our own minds and our own purposes, clearly expressed and boldly in conflict with another set of beliefs which, though they are supposed to be scientific, we have con-

ART AND THE ESCAPE FROM BANALITY

tracted rather than acquired, and which, half-unconsciously held, poison our minds and enfeeble our wills, as the body is weakened by some unknown septic source. And the first of these necessary beliefs I would state thus.

That reality itself is not something into which we are born and to which we are subject, but something which we have to achieve.

The next, closely connected with the first, is that this reality is not a mere caprice of our own, which we can create for ourselves and pursue by ourselves. For, just because reality is something we have to achieve, it follows that we can conceive it only more and more clearly as we achieve it. We are not, as many people suppose, who exult in the will and the wilful life, *selves* to start with. We have to achieve the self in achieving reality; and this self is something, as Plato would say, according to an eternal pattern, something already prophesied and potential in us, and something that cannot be satisfied or leave us happy except by the process of its own achievement.

From this it follows that reality for us is not in the past or in our origins, but in the future and in our aims; that if we would know what we are, we must try to discover what we desire to be. The individual, like the race, comes out of the undifferentiated: his past is a matter of knowledge; his future, of effort; and he must believe in effort as a fact more important, more real, than knowledge, because it is concerned with the process of differentiation, whereas knowledge is often concerned with the fact of sameness.

Hence we must not subject ourselves to the tyranny of science, of knowledge; we must assert, as being more real and even more true, the fact of effort, and we must see knowledge itself as subsidiary to that, never submitting

THE NECESSITY OF ART

our minds to the facts discovered about our own past; but saying to ourselves as an article of faith, and as a scientific statement even: " We are not what we have been but what we are trying to be."

And this for a very good reason; since in the undifferentiated past, whether of the race or of the individual, there is no self that can know either itself or anything else. Knowing even is part of the effort of the self to achieve itself, and, but for that effort, it would never have come into being; we should still be in the state of the amœba, which knows nothing about its own past or present or future.

But since reality and the self are something which we have to achieve, something which exists in an eternal pattern, but with which we have to identify ourselves, it follows that science, the knowledge of the past, the whole activity which concerns itself with knowing and observing, does not deserve the dangerous pre-eminence which it has gained among us, it is only part of a general effort, which must be general and balanced if we are even to learn the truth which science aims at, namely that morals are a part of that effort no less than science, and that art is a part of it as well.

I have insisted that there is in all human beings a continual desire for expression, which is part of the effort at differentiation, at the achievement of the self and of reality; and also that, where this desire is thwarted, suppressed or perverted, the victim of failure becomes actually that failure, is what he says in his effort to say something different; and this is what we might expect if the activity of art is on the same level with the moral and intellectual activities. For certainly we tend to become what we believe; and if there is error in our

ART AND THE ESCAPE FROM BANALITY

beliefs it enters into the very character. So, also, we tend to become what we do; and, if there is perversity or failure in our actions, it also enters into the very character. And so it is with art, and with all expression of ourselves at which we aim for the sake of expression. For that aim also is part of the effort to achieve ourselves. If I try to say something exactly, I am not trying to say what I have to say already. I am trying to make myself in saying it. The self, like the thing to be said, is in the future, it is something aimed at and not merely something to be discovered which already exists. That extreme differentiation of expression, at which the artist aims, is not, as some have vainly supposed, a differentiation of something already in his mind; it is rather a differentiation of the mind itself, which he has not yet achieved but is trying to achieve in the practice of his art. When Beethoven wrote a symphony, he was not writing down something which had already stamped itself on his mind, he was making himself as well as the symphony, becoming more and more precisely Beethoven as he achieved a more and more precise expression of Beethoven; he was in fact objectifying his achieved self; for the self will not achieve itself except by some kind of objectifying, by some greater precision in action. It must in some form make, or do, what it would be.

But these objectifications of art are monuments of the achieved self which give to all of us the delight of achievement and of what we call creation. In a great tune what we really feel is that there a self has for a moment prophetically achieved itself; for there it has said what could not be otherwise, there it has identified itself with the eternal pattern, and in doing so become at last com-

THE NECESSITY OF ART

pletely individual, escaping from the undifferentiated past into a future of complete reality which it shares with us all. It is like a bird let out of a cage and able to fly straight for Heaven; like an arrow from a bow aimed at the goal; and all these metaphors are inadequate, because it is the self and reality achieving itself in one process. Not only is the work of art being created, but the artist himself, and the universe with him.

One of the great discoveries of the nineteenth century was that art, the whole process of expression, is not a luxury but a necessity. It was made by Ruskin and Morris in their search for something which they felt to be lacking in the life of their time. They had become conscious of the fact, not merely that pictures or sculpture then were inferior to the pictures and sculpture of the Renaissance, but that civilized mankind were losing the power of expressing themselves in all that they did and made. Neither of these great men was a philosopher; but they felt the absence of expression, and the pretences of it, as positive ugliness; and they saw that ugliness was, not merely the lack of a luxury which a few connoisseurs had enjoyed in the past, but the symptom of a deep failure and perversity in the spirit of man. They were already prophetically troubled by that banality which now is troubling us all; Morris indeed foretold that it would be cumulative and must end in some great disaster. Art, he said, is the expression of the workman's pleasure in his work; and, if that pleasure is denied to him, sooner or later he will in some way and perhaps blindly take his revenge. We can now, perhaps, express his foreboding more precisely in psychological terms. Mankind, we can say, are committed to the process of expression, of differentiation. They cannot, for the sake of immediate

ART AND THE ESCAPE FROM BANALITY

power or comfort, reverse the process and try to be a herd or an army, without suffering quick spiritual and then material disaster through the suppression of desires which have become part of themselves and the very reasons why they wish to live. Individuals may not know why they are ill at ease, or what desire of theirs is unsatisfied, but the desire remains and, being suppressed, produces conduct which they do not understand, rages against they know not what, blind activities that only increase their causes, mental disorder that becomes endemic and collective. And, in fact, our whole society now spends its superfluous energies in activities which would seem to it insane if it were not so used to them and the causes of which it does not even attempt to understand. We are in the dangerous state of an individual who is controlled in the main by his unconscious, by desires of which he is unaware, and who finds reasons for his behaviour which are never the true reasons. Consider, for instance, the energy and money we spend on games and on watching them; on contests between prize-fighters, on horse-racing, and all kinds of gambling; on the means of rushing from place to place; and on substitutes for art, such as the cinema. We do not know why we do these things, we cannot analyse or account for the pleasure we get from them; we cannot even say whether the feeling aroused by them *is* pleasure. All we know is that we are like Blake's figure of a child which stretches out its hand and cries—" I want—I want." Without knowing what our wants are, we spend more and more money in satisfying them; and always the process becomes more and more expensive, being indeed valued because of its expense. An American writer, Mr Veblen, has written a book, *The Theory of the Leisured Classes*, in which he expounds

THE NECESSITY OF ART

what he calls the doctrine of conspicuous waste. It is that the rich wish to enjoy the fact of their riches, to give themselves a proof of their success; and that they do this by wasting money in conspicuous ways, the essence of the process, and its value for them, consisting in the fact that it is a waste which all can see. The doctrine is ingenious but imperfect, since it is not only the rich but all men, rich and poor, who indulge in conspicuous waste; our whole society is engaged in it. The tendency to waste is itself a symptom of unsatisfied desire; and Mr Veblen does not attempt to discover what that desire is. He sees mankind as necessarily irrational; art itself is for him a form of conspicuous waste; and he thinks that men can be made to behave rationally only by the pressure of immediate necessity. Free them from that; and they will begin automatically to indulge in conspicuous waste as the only manner in which they can enjoy their success in the struggle for life.

His book, in fact, is a counsel of despair because, behind his theory, there is little psychological knowledge or belief in psychology as a remedy. Perhaps there was something of the same despair in Ruskin and Morris and for the same reason. They were born before that psychological age which is now beginning and with which a new hope is already dawning upon us. For we go back to Blake, the prophet, and see hope even in unsatisfied desire; and, like Blake, we see that where there is unsatisfied desire, our task is not to suppress it, but to discover its object. Morris and Ruskin insisted too much on the wickedness of their age; they were too full of righteous indignation, which is merely the baffled emotion produced by an evil for which no remedy can

ART AND THE ESCAPE FROM BANALITY

be discerned. When you see people behaving with a perversity which is unintelligible to you because you do not know its causes, then the fact that you can do nothing with them provokes you to call them wicked and to punish them blindly for their wickedness, if you can. But the moment you begin to see the causes of their perversity, and so to have some hope of a remedy, your energy goes no longer into righteous indignation or punishment, but into the effort to find that remedy.

So now, perhaps, we begin to see the causes of all the conspicuous waste of our society, including our own; and we see also that it is vain to rail against it. We are all in the same boat; and what we have to do is to find the remedy by understanding ourselves and each other. Hitherto we have not been able to analyse the pleasure we get from different kinds of conspicuous waste; we cannot even say whether the feeling aroused by them is pleasure. But what we desire is pleasure; and it seems to me vain to deny that fact or to assert that it is wrong to desire it. The denial and the assertion come from the fact, not that pleasure is bad in itself, but that many people behave wrongly or foolishly in their pursuit of it. But this may be because, while desiring pleasure, they do not know how to get it—do not even know what it is. That this is so, I am convinced, from my observation both of myself and of others in the pursuit of it. There is indeed a kind of pleasure, always imperfect and unsatisfying, to be got from the pursuit of pleasure; and it is this secondary pleasure that most of us mistake for pleasure itself. We go expecting to enjoy something, and we do enjoy our expectation of enjoyment. But this enjoyment of expectation is something very different from direct enjoyment, which many of us never experience at

THE NECESSITY OF ART

all, except in the pleasure of the senses, or in some chance, wonderful moments which we can never recover—not knowing how or why they come. Now the pleasure of conspicuous waste, and of all the irrational amusements on which we spend so much of our energy, is, I am convinced, always this pleasure of expectation. Crowds assemble at a spectacle expecting pleasure; and they do enjoy that expectation, all the more because they are crowds of which each member believes that all the other members are enjoying themselves. But the enjoyment of expectation can never satisfy, and for that very reason, it makes more and more demands for greater elaboration and expense, hoping that, by those means, it will cease to be enjoyment of expectation and become the final satisfying enjoyment of the thing itself. A football audience thinks it will enjoy the game more if more money is paid to the players; or the audience at a prize-fight if the stakes are higher. And so people go to the opera even, which is supposed to be a form of art, because a prima donna is paid a thousand pounds for one performance. They expect, therefore, to enjoy her singing, but they enjoy only their expectation.

This, we know, is silly and vulgar; but we may not know why. The reason is that enjoyment of expectation never satisfies us; the more we have of it, the more we feel baulked and jaded. The very process indeed of enjoying expectation disappoints us; for there is always something beyond it, a different kind of pleasure, that we expect to enjoy but never attain to. Without the desire for this, we could not enjoy the expectation of it. But what is this further, direct pleasure, the very value of which makes us waste so much energy in enjoying the expectation of it? We know it, as I have said, in the

ART AND THE ESCAPE FROM BANALITY

pleasures of the senses and in those moments which happen by chance and which we cannot recover; and it is this knowledge that makes us hungry for direct pleasure and even for the expectation of it.

But as for the pleasures of the senses, we can never be satisfied with them. Our aim indeed is to carry pleasure into our other activities, to carry it from the body to the mind, and when we get a pleasure of the mind as direct as the pleasures of the body, then indeed we are satisfied. That, no doubt, is why mystics have used sexual images to express the union between the soul and God. They mean that there are pleasures of the mind, or spirit, as direct as the pleasures of the body, and far stronger, because the whole self consents to them utterly. But to get this direct pleasure of the mind is difficult; it is not given us like the pleasures of the body; we have to achieve it, both by discovering what will directly please the mind and by training the mind's capacity for that direct pleasure. For all of us pleasure of the mind consists, to start with, in expectation of bodily pleasure; and for many of us it remains that always. But this expectation of bodily pleasure may be cultivated as a pleasure in itself, may even be detached from any particular bodily pleasure that is expected, as in the case of voluptuous spectacles, all kinds of obscene art, and also scenes of vulgar splendour in the theatre or elsewhere. All such pleasures are, in the main, harmful, because they are red herrings which distract men from the pursuit of direct mental pleasure: for what they are worth, they are easily achieved, provided we are ready to waste our money on them; and in the long run they leave us dissatisfied. The appetite grows, not with the eating, but because there is nothing to eat.

THE NECESSITY OF ART

Yet the appetite may grow and make more and more demands, as it does now; games, spectacles, contests of all kinds, may become more and more expensive, always from the hope that if they cost more, the pleasure will be increased; and there will be only an increasing *malaise* in a public unaware what ails it or what it desires, namely that direct pleasure of the mind, which is less and less achieved, the more time and energy are given to the pleasures of expectation. The remedy is to be aware of the error, to distinguish between the pleasures of expectation and the direct pleasures of the mind, and to discover how the latter can be certainly obtained.

Now we know, or ought to know, that one of the means by which they can be obtained is art, both the practice and the experience of it. But this fact is hidden from us because we do not distinguish between real art which gives us this direct pleasure, and sham art which, at best, only gives us the pleasure of expecting some pleasure not really mental. Many people think, for instance, that a melodrama, which produces excitement and finally the gratification of a happy ending, is therefore art; or that a picture of a naked woman which excites desire is therefore art. All such errors are possible only to minds which have never experienced the direct pleasures of real art, a pleasure which has nothing to do with pretty women or happy endings, which may be given by tragedy, or a portrait of a plain old man, because it is a direct pleasure of the mind and not parasitic on pleasures of the body.

There is no way of knowing the direct pleasure of the mind except by experiencing it, for it cannot be described or defined in terms of other pleasures; but we need to be aware of its existence and supreme value, so that, when it happens to us, we may identify it and afterwards pursue

ART AND THE ESCAPE FROM BANALITY

it. Hence the need of tradition in the arts, which is now almost lost. The world has in the past discovered by experience that the direct pleasure of the mind is to be got from certain works of art, and that these have certain characteristics; also that the artists who produced them worked in a certain spirit, and that the public which enjoyed them came to them with certain expectations and with a certain attitude. It knew what to expect and what not to expect. It did not confuse pleasures of the mind with pleasures of the body; nor did it confuse the expectation of enjoyment with enjoyment itself. If there is to be a public for works of art, it must know certain things so well that it has no need to say them; it must have certain values firmly established in its mind. But this knowledge, those values, we have lost—though unconsciously we feel the need for them—and we can recover them only by a conscious effort. Above all, we must be ready to make sacrifices for art, even sacrifices of money. At present we have two false beliefs about art which almost prevent it from existing. One is that we can get it without paying for it; and the other is that, if it is good, it will in the long run pay for itself. But art cannot exist unless there is a public ready to pay for it at least as much as they pay for games; and this payment must be collective, as it has been whenever any form of art has been both secure and grandly practised. It is not merely the individual who expresses himself in terms of art or who can support it. A whole society must do both—in architecture, in drama, in music, in painting and in sculpture. Art in all its forms is the business of a civilized society, and is one of the proofs that it is a society and is civilized. A city can be made only by the harmony of the citizens; without that, you have London and our provincial towns. There is as much difference between them and true cities as between a mob and a choir. But this harmony can be accomplished only by a common desire for art strong enough to overcome individual greed, stupidity, and conceit. There must be in men's minds a pattern, as it were, of the city, of the whole life they wish to make, and a pattern which grows clearer in the making.

This pattern is not in our minds at present, because we make no effort to realize it; but the desire, in most of us unconscious, is there; and that desire must become aware of itself, must try to fulfil itself, if it is not to breed pestilence. The problem is not one imagined by wistful cranks who wish to be different from other men; it is real and practical. We find ourselves dull, and growing duller, in spite of our science and machinery and games and gambling. We have all the amusements that man can devise except the one that is most worth having, the only one that grows more amusing with its enjoyment and that connects pleasure with reality and God. Art makes the mind that enjoys it, as it makes the mind which produces it; it is both in the artist and in his audience a discovery of the self; it is differentiation by means of a trained harmony like that of players in an orchestra, who become completely themselves in a common desire and a common satisfaction.

This good at least has come of our loss of art, since it has happened in an age, not of general decadence, but of great intellectual and material energy,—that, becoming more and more aware of that loss, we are turning much of our intellectual energy to the questions: What is art? why have we lost it? and how shall we recover it? That is something which has never happened in past ages of artistic decadence. Not only have we conviction

ART AND THE ESCAPE FROM BANALITY

of sin, but we also begin to apply our scientific method to our sinfulness or impotence: we are not content to despair.

There are those who tell us, like Whistler, that art happens, and that we can do nothing to make it happen; the more we think about it the less we shall get it. But they argue from ages which did not think about it at all. The fact that we do think about it, and with growing intensity, is a new fact. History is not repeating itself in that matter. We are acquiring a mass of knowledge about it, not merely historical but also psychological and philosophic, which is new. That knowledge is a symptom of desire and should be, to judge by all analogies, a means of accomplishing desire.

No man can produce a work of art simply by taking thought; but, if the artistic faculty exists now as it always has existed, and also the faculty for understanding and enjoying art, then both are only hampered or destroyed by circumstances. There are obstacles in our own minds and in our external conditions of which we can, by the use of the intellect, become aware and which, by the same use, we can remove. Psychology cannot create selves but it can help us to know the selves we wish to be, and it can remove impediments which we ourselves through ignorance have set up to the achievement of our real desires. So, if only we can become aware that we have a strong and permanent though hitherto suppressed and concealed desire for art; if we can see that this desire is not trivial but a demand of our whole being; then the effort to produce art, now half-hearted and confused, will become clear and passionate; and, if at last art is achieved by that effort, it will be far more secure than ever in the past, for it will be protected by a knowledge of its enemies and dangers.

II
CHRISTIANITY AND ART

II

CHRISTIANITY AND ART

By Percy Dearmer

THE prevalent confusion on the subject of art is due not only to the lack of a simple philosophy of æsthetic, but also to a long-established historical mistake. It has been generally supposed that the religion of Christendom was fundamentally opposed to art, and that the Church had only taken art up as a plaything and a tool during a period, vaguely known as the Middle Ages, when her true character had been destroyed by corruption and superstition. Consequently the general notion among pious folk in the nineteenth century was that art was rather wrong, while the poets and artists of Europe generally considered that religion was rather stupid. On the one hand, even Ruskin, writing in 1851, said that he had "never yet met with a Christian whose heart was thoroughly set upon the world to come, and, so far as human judgment could pronounce, perfect and right before God, who cared about art at all."[1] The distrust passed away as the century drew towards its close; but to-day the religious world still looks upon art as a kind of furbelow, pleasurable and inexpensive, upon the real business of life—a view with which the business world cordially agrees, patronizing art with such gross maladroitness that the artist is more contemptuous than ever.

[1] *Stones of Venice*, 4th edition, 1886, vol. ii. p. 103. But Ruskin was only thirty-two when he wrote this, and it was doubtless true enough of the "religious world" in 1851.

THE NECESSITY OF ART

Shelley and Keats prophesied about beauty, with a new grasp of its intellectual content, at the time when the eclipse of the nineteenth century was beginning to cast its shadow over the architecture of the world. They showed their contempt for the official religion of their day by ignoring it. To them beauty was Greece, and art was something which had expired with the Roman Empire—as when Shelley, for instance, found nothing to look at in Ravenna but its classical remains. There followed a period when Christianity was supposed to have been the consistent enemy throughout of all beauty and joy. Swinburne [1] was but summing up a contemporary verdict of French literature when he put into the mouth of a Roman of the Constantinian age the words:—

> " Thou hast conquered, O pale Galilean ; the world has grown grey from thy breath ;
> We have drunken of things Lethean, and fed on the fullness of death . . .
> O lips that the live blood faints in, the leavings of rocks and soils !
> O ghastly stories of saints, dead limbs of gibbeted gods ! "

The contemporary French literature is full of the same idea : men assumed Christianity to be what the pictures and images of French churches proclaimed it. Mediæval monasticism and clericalism had indeed adopted an ascetic view of life, which was intensified by the Counter-Reformation and has overlaid the beauty of Continental churches with a morbid Puritanism more profound than anything to be found among Protestants. To men like Théophile Gautier, Christianity appeared as the enemy of that beauty which paganism was supposed to pro-

[1] Hymn to Proserpine, *Poems and Ballads*, First Series.

CHRISTIANITY AND ART

claim: "O vieux monde," he wrote in *Mademoiselle de Maupin*, "tout ce que tu as révéré est donc méprisé! ... De maigres anchorites ... de martyrs tout sanglants ... se sont juchés sur les piédestaux de tes dieux si beaux et si charmants. ... Le Christ a enveloppé le monde dans son linceul ... Virginité, plante amère, née sur un sol trempé de sang ... le monde antique ne te connaissait pas, fleur inféconde! ... Virginité, mysticisme, mélancholie, trois maladies nouvelles apportées par le Christ."[1]

John Addington Symonds[2] in his study of the Renaissance, which admirably sums up the opinion of his day, is obsessed with the same idea. Art to him is necessarily "sensuous," and Christianity ascetic; therefore every great artist, even a Giovanni Pisano or a Cimabue, has somehow to be dragged into the category of paganism and included in the Renaissance, with the remarkable historical result that "no true form of figurative art intervened between Greek sculpture and Italian painting" of the Renaissance.

Symonds indeed is an excellent representation of his age. He is torn between art and religion: both, he feels, are right; but he cannot reconcile them. He is "pagan" enough to appreciate the delight in things of beauty for their own sake; but he is still Puritan enough to be distrustful of plastic art and to use the word "sensuous" in two senses, ignoring the sacramental reconciliation between sense-form and spiritual idea which Hegel had taught, and which, after all, has been part of the philosophy of religion throughout the Christian

---
[1] Page 211 in the ordinary edition.
[2] *The Renaissance in Italy*: "The Fine Arts," 2nd edition, 1882, pp. 8, 13-39, etc.

era. He concludes his first chapter by saying that our deepest thoughts about the world and God cannot be personified by any æsthetic process, and therefore could never enter "that atmosphere wherein alone they could become through fine art luminous." The divinity in them "is a deity that refuses the investiture of form."

To this we can only say that art exists precisely to make our highest thoughts more "luminous"; and that, as a matter of plain history, Christianity has from the beginning demanded the investiture of form for its ideas, and, in Europe, of the human form.

It is significant that hardly anything was put forward from the theological side to meet these abundant misunderstandings. Westcott was perhaps the only theologian of importance who attempted to state a Christian philosophy of art, and this he only threw out in the form of an appendix, buried from the eyes of ordinary mortals in a work of Greek exegesis.[1] It is perhaps also significant that a writer so little in sympathy with the ecclesiological movement of his day should have got further than anyone else into the heart of the matter, as when he said that the object of art is "to present the truth of things under the aspect of beauty," that Christianity is "a transfiguration of all human powers by the revelation of their divine connexions and destiny," and that Christian art is "the interpretation of beauty in life under the light of the incarnation."

But unfortunately Westcott, like everybody else, thought that the Christian Church had started with an initial prejudice against art and that the evidence of

---

[1] Brooke Foss Westcott, *The Epistles of St John*, "The Greek Text," with Notes and Essays, 2nd edition, 1886. Appendix on *The Relation of Christianity to Art*, pp. 331-74.

CHRISTIANITY AND ART

history thus ran counter to his views. His essay therefore has helped to perpetuate errors which he accentuates in his desire to be fair to the other side. (1) He thought that Christianity had begun in an environment which was opposed to art because it was a Jewish environment. Without going aside into questions of Biblical chronology, we may assert with no fear of contradiction that the Hebrew religion had not been opposed to art, and that the Christian Church had no such environment to combat. (2) He thought that some of the earliest Christian writers condemned art. In every case it can be shown that it was not art that was condemned by them, but some misuse of it: even the intensely (and heretically) puritan Tertullian refused to admit—not the *artifices* but only the *artifices idolorum*.[1] (3) Christian arch-

[1] The view that the Early Church had set its face against the religious use of art was so confidently held in Protestant circles that for some time credence was refused to the discoveries of early Christian art in the Catacombs and elsewhere. The view was based upon the documents quoted by Westcott.
(1) A canon of the local Spanish synod of Elvira c. 303, had been made famous by Protestant controversialists, and is quoted by Westcott: it forbids pictures in the churches, "ne quod colitur et adoratur in parietibus depingatur," a curious inversion of language. Harnack (*Mission and Expansion of Christianity*, Eng. Trans. 1908, vol. ii. pp. 303-4) shows how exceptional this synod was, in the degradation which it vainly combated—murder, superstition, and incredible lechery among bishops and lay folk; exceptional also at that time in forbidding the marriage of the clergy, though the controversialists did not quote it on this head. There are two other instances which Westcott gives. (2) Eusebius of Cæsarea († c. 339) wrote to the Empress Constantia that images of Christ are forbidden and that he had disapproved of an image of Paul. This is an instance of the Eastern aversion to images which led in the eighth century to the iconoclastic controversy. It does not represent any opposition to art, for Eusebius loves describing the magnificence of Christian churches. The iconoclastic emperors were also great patrons of art in general. (3) Epiphanius († 403) tore asunder a veil "bearing a fanciful image of Christ or of some saint" in a village church in Palestine. Images of Christ and of the saints were common, none the less, in the times of Epiphanius and Eusebius, both in Constantinople and Rome. Perhaps I may add that I have great sympathy with these early

THE NECESSITY OF ART

æology was still in its youth when Westcott wrote. He thought that the Catacombs of Rome were exceptional in their art and that their chronology was uncertain. We now know that similar art with the same iconography existed all over Mediterranean Christendom; and the various frescoes are now dated to within half a century or less.

Before we proceed to look a little further into the historical evidence, we may sum up the present misunderstanding by saying that it is due to ignorance caused by:—

1. The absence of any traditional philosophy. The very word "æsthetic" was only given its present meaning by Baumgarten in 1750, and it was dragged in the mud during the last quarter of the nineteenth century. The world has had its working rules of conduct in short axioms, creeds and catechisms; but it has had no catechism of æsthetic principles. In this we have been less fortunate perhaps than China, where the Zen doctrine did give the artist a spiritual principle,—the idea that art is a kind of Zen, or digging down to the divine within us; that it is in fact one form of the meditation and mental concentration whereby men obtain access to that part of their nature which is universal and divine. Many artists in the West must have felt this, and said it; but it was not codified for the multitude, any more than were the main principles of Hegel's "Æsthetic."

2. The confusion of the Christian tradition caused

opponents of such images. The maudlin misrepresentations of Christ in contemporary religious art make one wish that nothing of the kind had ever been allowed. That so much traditional religion is Docetic, regarding Christ as not really human, is largely due to bad art. At the same time it may be true that Christianity would not have succeeded in converting Europe if representations of Christ had been forbidden altogether.

CHRISTIANITY AND ART

by the hardening of mediæval thought under monastic influence; and the consequent classical and Hebraistic reactions of the fifteenth and sixteenth centuries, which have continued down to our own time.

3. The almost complete ignorance of both early Christian and Byzantine art, even among Church historians, and, by contrast with this, the universal teaching of classical iconography in the schools of Europe, from generation to generation.

4. The consequent ignorance of the development of art during the Christian era, and especially of the enormous difficulties, due to the break-up of the Imperial system of ancient Rome, which were encountered and gradually overcome.

We must therefore speak at rather more length about the surviving examples of that early Christian art which was produced in the two hundred and fifty years before Constantine.

Asia

For the reader's sake, we will avoid the complications involved in a discussion of the Farther East and confine ourselves to Mediterranean Christendom—the usual area of the historian. But in so doing we must not forget that we are ignoring about two-thirds of the territory. The early Church spread rapidly over Mesopotamia and Persia (reaching ultimately to Chinese Turkestan, and even to China, as well as to South India) : in the Persian Empire the Church enjoyed complete freedom during the time that she was being persecuted in that of Rome: Armenia became a Christian state before Constantine began the Christianization of the Roman Empire. The art of this vast Iranian area had always been non-

THE NECESSITY OF ART

representational; and, when Christianity arrived, it was expressed by symbols and not by figure-art. Strzygowski is doubtless right in stating, as a result of thirty years' excavations, that the real cradle of Christian art lies about the Tigris and Euphrates and in the regions beyond: this art gave us the dome and the vault, mainly by way of Antioch and Constantinople (S. Sofia itself being really an Armenian church), and through its impact with the Northern races became the parent of the so-called Romanesque and Gothic architectures. Therefore, although we are now to consider the art of Europe, we must remember that Greco-Roman art was only a branch—and at the time was a subsidiary branch—of the art of that religion which, beginning in Syria, spread to the " Parthians, Medes, Elamites, dwellers in Mesopotamia," more rapidly than to the Empire of the West. From the evolutionary point of view, the art of the Roman Catacombs has little value, because it was not the germ of Christian art, but the last stage of Greco-Roman art; but as evidence of the Christian spirit in art it is of immense value, and it is all that remains extant in any freshness or abundance.

Pre-Constantinian Art

The world at the beginning of our era was in great need of moral reform, but it was not (as it is to-day) corrupted by ugliness, and it did not begin to show signs of marked æsthetic decadence till the second century. The infant Church concentrated its energies on moral reform; but it did not neglect art. Accepting the Greco-Roman art of the time the Church in the

CHRISTIANITY AND ART

Mediterranean area accompanied that art through its decline till the age of Constantine, and then with increasing power effected a remarkable recovery. Since the Roman Catacombs were rediscovered in 1578 and systematically explored and photographed in recent years, it has been established that several examples of Christian painting exist which belong to the period when the Gospels were being written.

These Gospels are necessarily taken up with urgent moral and religious questions, but they are singularly pictorial in character, and they give us glimpses of the Founder of Christianity, which show him not only as a great Reformer, but also as a human being without the usual limitations of the reformer, full of imagination, insight, poetry. It is good to know that he sang, that he was once deeply moved by the architecture of the Temple, and once by its desecration, that he was deeply moved also by the sight of a town spreading out at his feet, that he defended, against Judas, the "waste" of money on a beautiful act, that he loved to withdraw himself into the silent influences of Nature, that he noticed with an intimate sympathy the flowers and the birds, and that he was the first man on record to proclaim the loveliness of little children. He thought in pictures and he taught in pictures; he had the mind of a poet, and some of his sayings have come down to us in definite poetic form. He presented ethics to the world under the aspect of beauty, and he made his followers think of God in the new and lovely way of a very human Father, and of himself as the ποιμὴν ὁ καλός—the Beautiful Shepherd. They have since distorted his teaching in many ways, but they have never ceased to think of saintliness in terms of beauty (the very word χάρις, "grace,"

THE NECESSITY OF ART

means loveliness and delight), nor ever forgotten to picture heaven as the place where

> "In that land of beauty
> All things of beauty meet."

The commentary supplied by those remaining frescoes in the Catacombs, which are of the apostolic and sub-apostolic era, give us the same impression. Painted by torchlight in the gloom of these confined and terrifying chambers, they are as free from the sadness of pagan funereal art as from the horror of damnation which was fastened upon the Christian art of a later period. They are funereal; yet they bring the light of the gay life above—birds and flowers, garlands and landscapes, winged genii and *putti*—down to the chambers of the dead. There is indeed no thought of death, and hardly a sign that many who lay there had met the death of martyrs. The tiny chapels, made only for memorial purposes, are so gaily decorated that, were their white plaster and bright wreaths copied in a modern church, the congregation would say: "They have made our church look like a theatre"; and were these admirable decorations used to supplant the stolid gilding of a London theatre, the critics would say : " The influence of the Russian ballet is spreading into the auditorium." It was the Greco-Roman art of the period which the first Christians used, employing doubtless the ordinary craftsmen of the city,[1] since the burying-places of Christians were protected by

---

[1] The artists of Rome were mostly Greek, but there was also a strong Alexandrian influence. The Church throughout Italy was also mostly Greek; only two bishops of Rome before Victor (189-199) have Latin names.

law, even when their persons were not. But they used this art with a difference: they purged it of objectionable features, such as can still be seen in Pompeii to-day, and they chose such objects as were not purely decorative with a definite symbolical meaning. There exist examples of the latter part of the first century—Daniel between two heraldic-looking lions (as a type of deliverance); a fisherman, a lamb, and three pictures of the Good—the "Beautiful"—Shepherd, always a fair, beardless youth, dressed as a shepherd of the Campagna, in a short tunic, sometimes with a staff, and sometimes playing upon the pipes.

In the extant work of the second and third centuries, spread among the five hundred miles of the Roman Catacombs, the subjects are multiplied, and there appears a certain amount of *genre* painting; but their character is little changed. The style is that of the age, but the character is always unmistakably Christian,—blithe, tender, symbolical. Orpheus sometimes appears as a type of Christ, and the Good Shepherd is sometimes shown surrounded by his flock, a subject which becomes more common in the fourth century.

We are compelled to estimate the art of this first period rather by its subject-matter than by its technique; for the painters employed must have been drawn at first from the ordinary pagan workshops where the guilds of the period worked under their Greek guild-masters. But there is an absolute distinction from the beginning, not only in the spirit, the marked use of symbolism, and the general iconography, but also in the composition of early Christian painting; for, whereas Greco-Roman art was increasingly crowded with "superfluous and useless additions," the painting in the Catacombs always

THE NECESSITY OF ART

avoids the massing together of figures and concentrates on the simple elements of each scene.[1]

It is commonly assumed that all early Christian art was funereal in character; but we have no right to make the assumption. The painting that has survived is funereal because the Catacombs have survived—if indeed the epithet funereal may be applied to work so astonishingly cheerful and in such striking contrast with the funereal art of later times; but the early Christians did not live in the Catacombs, nor did they worship in the Catacombs except at memorial services. They lived above ground like other people, and they worshipped at first in the *atria* of private houses, then in what Harnack calls hall-churches; and long before Constantine they had large churches of their own. "The Christians," complained Porphyry, who was born in 233, "in rivalry of our temples, build very large houses ($\mu\epsilon\gamma\acute{\iota}\sigma\tau o \upsilon\varsigma$ o$\mathring{\iota}\kappa o\upsilon\varsigma$) where they assemble to pray."

Diocletian ordered the destruction of all churches throughout the Empire; but the churches in Rome condemned by him in 300 were not after all destroyed, for Maxentius restored them in 311 to the Bishop Miltiades; and we know that about the year 315 there were over forty basilicas in the city.[2] But, alas! we can only imagine the art of these Christian homes and churches: the amazing wealth of vessels and candelabra, which Con-

---

[1] A. della Seta, *Religione e arte figurata*, 1912. Professor della Seta must, however, be mistaken in attributing the carelessness of some of the later work to religious reasons. Underground painting tends to be careless, and the general art of the time was deteriorating in the third century.

[2] P. Batiffol, *La Paix constantinienne*, 1914, p. 177; *La Messe*, 1919, p. 47; A. Harnack, *Mission und Ausbreitung*, 1915, II. Appendix to chap. ii. Harnack attributes the hall-churches mainly to the second century, and the early basilicas to the almost unbroken period of peace between 160 and 203.

CHRISTIANITY AND ART

stantine gave a few years later, help us to form a general idea of what the more frugal ornament had been in the third century; for custom is conservative in such matters, and the documents show that a considerable ceremonial had grown up by the end of the second century. As for the art of people's houses, we have one or two clues—the statuettes of the Good Shepherd, for instance, many engraved gems from the second century onwards, tapestries in Egypt from the third, and the patrician house of the Martyrs John and Paul on the Cælian hill, which show that the homes of upper-class Christians were decorated in the same style as those of pagans. Most significant perhaps of all were the innumerable glass vessels found in the Catacombs, especially those in gold-glass—a third and fourth century art, almost entirely associated with Christianity—which are decorated with the same religious subjects as the Catacombs themselves; and also with pictures of saints, especially Peter and Paul, with very many *genre* subjects (a carpenter's shop, for example), and with representations of a married pair or a family group. Many of these were doubtless wedding or birthday presents; and many bear the usual toasts, *Pie zeses*—"Drink and Live!" or "Take a crown, drink and live!" We need not assume, then, that these Christians only knew how to die.

BASILICAN ART

From the third century, Greco-Roman civilization had been consciously decadent, in statecraft, education, literature and art. Christianity came into power during the fourth century, too late to save the Empire, but not too late to reconstruct civilization. Already, by the year 400, the Goths were crossing the Danube, pushed southward by the more desperate savagery of the Huns from Asia. In 410 Alaric sacked Rome. Thenceforward till the rise of Romanesque art in the middle of the Christian era, the condition of Europe may be described in a sentence. Wave after wave of barbarians swept over Europe—Goths, Vandals, Lombards, Franks, Burgundians, Angles, Saracens, Vikings—while Constantinople alone remained inviolate within its shrinking territories: the Church survived each merciless conquest, mitigated its horrors, tamed, converted, and gradually civilized the conquerors.

She had strengthened herself for the task after the formal recognition of 313, when she ceased to be a proscribed sect; and the result of that new power is written in the basilican churches of Constantine's reign. Those in Byzantium disappeared long ago, but superb examples in Rome still exist, though old S. Peter's, Constantine's greatest church, was pulled down in the sixteenth century.

There is a remarkable change in this new ecclesiastical work. The last buildings of pagan Rome are unwaveringly Roman: Diocletian's baths, the basilica so-called of Maxentius, which Constantine finished in his own name, the triumphal arch which also bears his name, decadent though they are, show no trace of any new development. Constantine the statesman built in the old style: but in the work of Constantine the Christian there is an absolute break, a complete change of type. Without a sign of any transition, the imperial basilican church appears in Rome.

No doubt the explanation is that the Emperor was copying those older basilican churches which had existed, as we have said, since the second century, and were an

CHRISTIANITY AND ART

adaptation of the Hellenistic timber-roofed hall, with some elements perhaps derived from domestic architecture. The basilican church was excellently adapted to the requirements of the new faith. It had no relationship with the temples of the pagan religions, for these were houses of the gods and not built for congregational worship: the sacrifice was made on the threshold of the temple, not within, and the worshipper saluted with a gesture. The basilica, on the other hand, was a home where many people could assemble together for worship—already in the third century it is called *domus ecclesiæ*—and there were generally smaller rooms grouped about it. It expressed the unity of the people as they stood in the great nave before the altar, which was ringed about with deacons, and behind which the bishop presided, sitting in the apse where the higher clergy were placed around him in a semicircle.

Christianity differed from paganism in being a religion of fellowship, requiring great congregational services. Its immediate need had been a large building, lightly constructed and freed from the tyranny of the entablature, protected from the weather by the simplest of walls and roofs, its ornament concentrated on the interior. Such was the basilica—of a long, rectangular plan, with a courtyard, narthex, nave, and apse, and with single or double aisles, where (in spite of the curtains that came to be hung between the columns), large numbers of people could assist. The basilican style was unprogressive, excellently suited, as it happened, to hold its own through the difficult ages that were to follow. After a thousand years had passed, basilicas were still built in some places; indeed Brunellesco's two great so-called Renaissance churches at Florence, begun in 1430, are but basilicas

THE NECESSITY OF ART

with a dome at the crossing, like Pisa Cathedral, which was begun in 1063. But for the most part the basilican style in Italy passed through Byzantinesque almost insensibly into Romanesque; though the basilica has never ceased to supply the general plan upon which Christian churches are built. The basilica was the European contribution to Christian architecture; the dome and the vault were the Asiatic contributions from Armenia and Persia, and from Mesopotamia respectively.

In painting, the fourth century brought about a marked change, at least so far as the iconography is concerned: the transition can be studied in the Catacombs, where painting is continued through the Constantinian era. The symbolism becomes more obvious, more dogmatic, and less mystical; more ecclesiastical, more didactic, and less religious. This is best illustrated by a single fact: the Good Shepherd disappears, and is replaced by the imperial Despot, a figure in type and costume recalling the images of Augustus himself.

Art is expression, and it expresses among other things the conditions and the mentality of those who use it. Art, in fact, is an interpreter of history, and it is only a misconception either of history or of art that has caused some writers to ignore or deny this fact. Christian art before Constantine was democratic, in the sense that it expressed the ideas of the people, but let us drop the overstrained word "democratic" and say that Christian art was *vernacular*. The Good Shepherd never was popular among theologians and church-authorities until the nineteenth century: he is hardly mentioned even in the earliest Christian writings. But the people loved him: and the Church is not the theologians, nor the bishops, nor the other clergy, but the whole Christian

CHRISTIANITY AND ART

community. Once or twice in history the Christian community has become vocal and has expressed itself. There was thus a modest vernacular art in the Early Church—in the little-known Churches of Asia, as in Rome—a magnificent vernacular art in the Gothic period, and another in Florence, at least from the time of Giotto to that of Botticelli, when the people were not dictated to from above.[1] The religion of the Early Church—not in Rome only but everywhere—was the religion of the Good Shepherd. Then came the gradual establishment of Christianity in the West under Constantine, bringing much good both in life and in art; but it took away the Good Shepherd.

A new form of Christianity became paramount, hierarchic in its life, hieratical in its art. Byzantinism follows—again bringing much good with it and creating a magnificent art; but its Christ is the Pantokrator of the great mosaics, the awful ruler and judge, not the Beautiful Shepherd; and its subject-matter is neither the cheerful symbolism of the Early Church, nor the balder Constantinian record of Old and New Testament history, but the Kalendar of the Eastern Church. Art, in fact, became imperial, dogmatic, ecclesiastical, and iconolatrous. It expressed exactly the thought and life of the time.

In sculpture there was during the Constantinian era a dovetailing of the old Greco-Roman art with the new Christian art in the Hellenistic tradition. Christian sculpture had existed in the West before Constantine, in spite of the danger of idolatry: a few sarcophagi of the third century survive and of the eight statuettes of the

---

[1] See Wilhelm Bode, *Florentine Bildhauer der Renaissance*, 1902, cap. I. Florentine art survived the Medicean usurpation for fifty years.

THE NECESSITY OF ART

Good Shepherd which have been found, the one at the Lateran (attributed to the third century) is of singular grace and charm. Most of the extant Christian sculpture is upon sarcophagi (which have a high survival value) and, because the carving of sarcophagi was a flourishing trade at the time, there was at first no distinction between pagan and Christian examples, except in the subject-matter. They were just ordered at the shops. But already by the time of Constantine a definitely Christian style appears at Ravenna, in the beautiful sarcophagi with animated distinctive figures, as different as possible from the crowded reliefs of the traditional Greco-Roman style.

Meanwhile Greco-Roman sculpture, which had been declining in the second and third centuries, continued on the down-grade. Coinage especially grows very unequal, sometimes of perfect execution, sometimes barbarously bad, especially between the sixth and eighth centuries, though we must not judge the art of a period entirely by its coinage, unless we are prepared to have the England of to-day estimated by its pennies or its postage-stamps. Side by side with the declining Greco-Roman sculpture, the new Christian work develops, but it is Byzantine in character: the influence of the lands on the far borders of the Eastern Empire—Persia and Mesopotamia—was already penetrating the Hellenistic world, and that influence was decorative and strongly against the plastic representation of the human form. Byzantine art, therefore, tended to confine itself to sculpture in relief; figure-sculpture on a large scale declined during the fourth and fifth centuries and had become exceptional in the age of Justinian.

CHRISTIANITY AND ART

Byzantine Art

There is no need to dwell on Byzantine architecture, since everyone now recognizes that it is one of the most glorious inventions in the history of mankind. All our Western domes are the children of S. Sofia, where the art of Asia comes to the succour of the art of Europe; and S. Sofia is, as William Morris said, the finest building in the world. That wonderful creation had many sisters in Constantinople, each full of originality, some of which have also escaped destruction. Byzantine churches hardly less fine are still to be found in the Balkan Peninsula, and, with a difference, in Sicily. S. Mark's at Venice is a purely Byzantine church, copied in the eleventh century from the Church of the Apostles at Constantinople (since destroyed); and Byzantine churches cover the vast area of Russia to-day, from the Baltic to the sea of Japan.

Painting, the specifically Christian art of painting with cubes of coloured glass upon large wall surfaces, is another undisputed glory of the Byzantine genius. Glass mosaic springs at once into perfection with the earliest examples we possess: those of Constantine, Theodoric, Justinian, at Rome and Ravenna, are among the greatest works of art that man has produced; and in them also the ideas of Asia are blended with those of Europe. Mosaic flourished for a thousand years, and if it changed but little, this was because there was but little room for change: nothing could improve, for instance, the colour and design of the pictures in S. Vitale or S. Apollinare Nuovo, and what is left at S. Sofia shows that the work there was not inferior. In nearly all the examples—in Europe, Western Asia and North Africa, all round the Mediterranean—there

THE NECESSITY OF ART

is the same splendid simplicity of design, the same shimmering, glowing, dusky glory of colour. We can understand why, until the thirteenth century, painting in fresco or tempera was regarded as a cheap substitute for painting in stained and gilded glass, and is a sign in a great city like Rome of weakness and distress in contemporary history.

The surviving mosaics and frescoes show how profoundly mistaken is the idea that there was no great painting before Cimabue. Intervals of weakness there were;[1] but there was no gap:—from the Catacombs, from the great mosaics of the fourth and sixth centuries to those of the eleventh at Daphni in Attica, S. Luke in Phocis, and Torcello; or to the noble frescoes of that period at S. Clemente in Rome; or to the mosaics at S. Mark's, Venice, from the eleventh to the thirteenth and fourteenth centuries; or those of the twelfth century in Sicily, and of the fourteenth in what is now the Kahrié Djami Mosque at Constantinople: and, side by side with the monumental painting there run like a commentary all through this millennium the fine miniatures of innumerable manuscripts, which counteracted the tendency to immobility and isolation of the wall-pictures, and kept alive the tradition of action by their representation of narrative subjects.[2]

---

[1] As at S. Apollinare in Classe, Ravenna, in the seventh century; and generally, so far as we know, in the eighth. In Rome we have no mosaics between c. 710 and c. 800, but the discovery of S. Maria Antiqua has revealed some frescoes, and we know that Gregory III (731-41), the opponent of the Iconoclasts, patronized the painters. In mosaic again there is a decline after S. Nereo ed Achilleo (c. 800), in S. Prassede (817-24), and more marked in S. Maria in Domnica. There are frescoes of c. 850 at S. Clemente, in the vivacious Carolingian style of the North, and good Byzantine work of the tenth century at S. Elia, Nepi.

[2] As this whole matter is but little known, it may be as well to give a list here of some typical surviving examples: 4 *Cent.*: Mosaics; Rome, S. Costanza (A.D. 330), S. Pudenziana (c. 395). 5 *Cent.*: Rome, S. Maria

CHRISTIANITY AND ART

Sculpture, as we have said, in the fourth century recovered from its decline, and developed under the inspiration of the artistic influence brought by the Church from the Eastern Empire. This sculpture was the direct descendant of Hellenistic art, but it was modified by the aversion to human representation which came into Byzantium from the Asiatic side. Henceforward, sculpture was in relief and on a small scale, such as that of the admirable fifth-century doors of S. Sabina, or the beautiful ivory diptych of some fifty years or so later (Adam in Eden and St Paul at Malta), now in the Bargello at Florence, or the many other examples of less distinction.

It was fortunate for Europe that Byzantine sculpture continued to be on a small scale for the next thousand

Maggiore (perhaps by Syrian artists. Some of the work may be earlier); Lateran Baptistery. 6 *Cent.*: The great mosaics of Ravenna; Rome, S. Cosma e Damiano; Parenzo in Istria. 6-8 *Cent.*: Salonika, S. Demetrius and S. Sofia. 7 *Cent.*: (the most ancient mosaics of Palestine have been destroyed, but the monastery of S. Catherine on Mount Sinai is probably 7 Cent.); Rome, mosaics at S. Agnese, S. Venanzio. 8 *Cent.*: last frescoes in the Catacombs; S. Maria Antiqua. 9 *Cent.*: Rome, mosaics at S. Prassede, etc.; Nicæa, Church of the Koimesis. 10 *Cent.*: Rome, frescoes, S. Maria in Pallaria; Nepi, S. Elia; Oberzell in Reichenau. For a MS. example, the Paris Psalter: there was an original Anglo-Saxon school of miniaturists (c. 950-1100), influenced by Egypt and Syria. 11 *Cent.*: Great mosaics at Daphni; Torcello; S. Mark's, Venice; and S. Sofia, Kiev; Roman frescoes at S. Urbano alla Caffarella, and the famous examples at S. Clemente; S. Savin, Vienne, France. 12 *Cent.*: Apse mosaics of S. Clemente; S. Maria in Trastevere, and S. Maria Nuova, Rome. 13 *Cent.*: mosaics at S. Mark's continue. Painters: Giunta da Pisa, painting in 1202; Coppo di Marcovaldo in 1261; Guido da Siena in 1271; Cimabue in Rome, 1272; Duccio in 1278; Cavallini in 1280; Giotto at Assisi, c. 1295. Mosaicists: Cimabue, Cavallini, Giotto; Torriti and Rusuti in Rome, 1291-5. 14 *Cent.*: Giotto dies, 1336; Simone Martini, the Lorenzetti, etc. 15 *Cent.*: Masaccio, Botticelli, etc., early work of Michelangelo, etc.

Since the above was in type, there has appeared a monumental work by Wilpert, *Die Römischen Mosaiken und Malereien der Kirchlichen Bauten vom IV bis XIII Jahrhundert* (Herder, Freiburg i. B.). The extent of his record may be gathered from the fact that there are 300 coloured plates, with 542 other illustrations, and that the book costs £140.

THE NECESSITY OF ART

years, until the fall indeed of Constantinople at a time when Donatello and his fellow-craftsmen had nothing more to learn; because the birth of sculpture in France and Italy was due, mainly, to the portable Byzantine ivories.

The influence of Constantinople, which remained unconquered during this thousand years and went through no dark ages, is in fact the key to the understanding of mediæval art. Throughout the difficult era when the barbarians were being educated, Byzantine miniatures and ivories, spreading westward along the trade-routes, kept the memory of art alive, and gradually effected its recovery. Sculpture is the most difficult art for uneducated races to appreciate: the Gaulish soldiers had shouted with laughter at the sight of the statues of Delphi; and we have barbaric sculpture in Gaul down to the end of the tenth century—huge feet and hands, large eyes in the middle of the temple, noses more than half the length of the face, and ears like jug-handles. Till the year 1000, European art can be classified under two heads, Byzantinism and Barbarism.

This Byzantine maternity is still insufficiently realized. For this long millennium, until its capture by the Turks in 1453, Constantinople continued to be the chief centre both of learning and of art. The other great cities were children of the city that stood on the frontier between Asia and Europe. Ravenna was already Byzantine when it became the new capital of the shrinking Western Empire. Rome was a Greek city from the sixth to the ninth century—the Rome, for instance, to which our English Benedict Biscop sent for his pictures and his music. Calabria and Apulia were colonized by Greek monks from the ninth to the eleventh century. Italian archi-

CHRISTIANITY AND ART

tecture became Byzantinesque between the sixth and eleventh centuries, before it was Romanesque. Venice was for seven centuries a great Byzantine city. It was the Greek monks of South Italy who had supplied his models to Duccio: Byzantine art made the work of Cimabue possible, and lay behind the discoveries of Giotto.

Thus, until Europe began to settle down in the eleventh century, art was kept alive and developed all over Europe by the Christian nations of the East, and was fostered and encouraged by the monks of the West. The "harsh, emaciated," and "Lethean" look of some earlier mediæval art which has so often been laid to the charge of Christianity, is simply due to the fact that the full-blooded young races in the West had not yet acquired the necessary technique. So far from the Church being opposed to the human form, she required that form, as we have already said, for the teaching of her doctrines, because her message was the incarnation of divinity, and because she knew what some modern painters tend to forget—that you cannot represent the soul of man without some adequate representation of his body. Before their conversion Goths and Celts alike had an art which was purely decorative, intricate combinations of line, which had little message for the soul: it was Christianity that established a higher art among the barbarians, because it gave them a religion to which the presentation of the human form was essential.[1]

It was not the fault of Gibbon or Grote, or our grandfathers, that they knew nothing of all this: travel was difficult in their day, the East was almost inaccessible, excavation had hardly begun; comparative study was

[1] See O. M. Dalton, *Byzantine Art and Archæology*, 1911, pp. 25-6.

THE NECESSITY OF ART

impossible before the invention of photography. But there is no excuse for us if we continue to think in these categories. Every year we are making fresh discoveries even in Rome itself : Constantinople is only now coming within reach of scientific examination : Asia Minor and Syria have had little more than a preliminary survey ; the all-important land in North Mesopotamia, now called Diarbekir, still awaits excavation. Yet we have already discovered that Romanesque architecture is indebted in a surprising degree to the Christian East—to Mesopotamia, to Syria, where have been discovered hundreds of remarkable churches of the fourth and fifth centuries, laid waste by the first fury of Islam, and to Armenia, where a later but not less remarkable architecture lies in the wilderness of a later desolation.

Romanesque and Gothic

Of Romanesque and Gothic art we need not speak at any length. In the former, the young races had come into their strength, still under monastic tutelage : in the latter, they express their full humanity, freely, turbulently, and yet with a singular precision of logical science. There was never anything before at all like the amazing vitality with which Romanesque, already flourishing in many varied forms, developed into one style of Gothic after another, each original and audacious, following natural laws and developing natural ornament. Gothic differs from all other architecture in its naturalism, its freedom, its growth ; it differs from all except Byzantine in its daring and romance ; it introduced into the art of building the new principles of elasticity and luminosity. Interrupted for a few centuries by an eruption

CHRISTIANITY AND ART

of pedantry, discredited in the nineteenth century by an imitation not less pedantic, the Gothic spirit was rediscovered in the scientific doctrine of evolution; and the Gothic principle of building—its soaring audacity, its forward-looking, democratic liberty—will be the principle of all building in the future, whether in steel or stone, timber or concrete. Yet the parent Romanesque was so noble that we can hardly pardon Gothic for leaving it behind.

Both styles of architecture spring from the same practical and very significant source. The disappearance of slave-labour had made it impossible to build in the classical manner with huge blocks of stone: from this necessity of using stones which one man could handle, Romanesque architecture arose, and the mason became a free man and an artist.

The Development in Iconography and the Triumph of Humanism

The subject-matter of Byzantine painting and sculpture continued in the East with little change until the fifteenth century, when the prospect of a great development similar to that of Italy was destroyed by the fall of Constantinople. In the West, after the long barbaric interlude, monasticism dictated the didactic iconography of the Romanesque period—Christ, suffering or triumphant, stories of the saints, and the Last Judgment (to frighten the evil-doer). During the Gothic period art became again vernacular; and, though the clergy continued to use the devils of the Last Judgment to assist them in their difficult work of taming our ancestors, there is a very wonderful extension of figurative art, and the calm

THE NECESSITY OF ART

radiance of Gothic statuary includes the personification of all the known arts and sciences, and is surrounded by every kind of lovely natural form. The art of the thirteenth century is at once strenuous and serene, confident and tender, lofty and gay.

In the fourteenth century, when France is at the depth of her miseries, the old cheerful confidence is gone : an ingratiating air is noticeable in the Madonnas of a Church that is being questioned and has embarked on persecution. A wave also of sadness sweeps over West Christian art, and the Black Death emphasizes a morbid sentimentalism, rejoicing in the *macabre*, in tears and blood, which has not yet to-day been shaken off : S. Francis has already popularized the crucifix, and scenes from the Passion replace the legends of the saints upon the carved altar-pieces. France, torn by faction and wasted by invasion, has lost the lead which she had held since the first beginnings of Gothic art.

The torch passes to Italy, where humanism and realism become powerful in the hands of the Gothic painters and sculptors, Giotto, Giovanni Pisano, and their contemporaries. But during the fourteenth century an enthusiasm for classical antiquity grows up, and gradually makes itself felt in architecture and sculpture, and then in painting ; so that by the end of the fifteenth century artists like Mantegna, Botticelli and Pietro di Cosimo are painting mythological subjects. These men are Christians—one of them takes part in the revivalism of Savonarola—but they are also sharers in a revolt. What has happened ?

The Intellectual Revolution has begun, and humanism is overthrowing mediævalism. For long, the clergy had made art extremely didactic : the rest of the Church,

CHRISTIANITY AND ART

the laity, had agreed in this; for the Church indeed was still the whole Christian community, and a man like Giotto was as anxious to paint the story of S. Francis and the ecclesiastical cycle from the Gospels and from the apocryphal legends of Mary, as the clergy were to have them painted. But a century after Giotto's death, the Church which is the whole company of Christian people is less identified with the clergy. The old subjects have ceased to be adequate; the morbid sadness which had overspread Gothic art in fourteenth-century France has little echo in Italy, where during the same era there has been arising a joy in life which is often imagined to be pagan but is really of the very essence of New Testament Christianity.

For indeed Christianity, after the anchorite passion which followed the settlement of Constantine, had never been entirely free from that common disease of religion —asceticism. In spite of the fact that Christ had taught, not asceticism but health, and had actually been attacked because he ate and drank like other people, there had crept over Christendom the old cult of suffering, which has its roots in the old ideas of the cruelty of the gods. Asceticism had never become the religion of the people as a whole, but it was the ideal of many of the most devoted communities and individuals: and it was widely proclaimed by the ecclesiastical authorities, although in strict theology it was only regarded as one way, and not necessarily a better way, of serving God.

Humanism was the revolt of the educated layman against ecclesiastical restraint. The Church had educated a large number of people, and naturally enough wanted to retain the leading-strings: this became increasingly difficult as the book gradually supplanted the battle-axe;

THE NECESSITY OF ART

the upper classes began to look for larger fields of life, for wider knowledge, for *literæ humaniores*. By the end of the fourteenth century, Humanism had become powerful; but it had originated long before: it goes back indeed behind Petrarch to Marsiglio of Padua, to Dante, to Frederic II, to S. Francis even, and behind him to the Albigenses, and the troubadours, and to Abélard.

Humanism is the product of the second millennium of Christian history; and it has increased in power to the present day.

The Classical Revival was a sequel to Humanism, supplying that core of reaction which is to be found in all revolutions. It has been an illuminative but never a creative movement, and is at the present day a brake upon the energy of natural science. Men who desire change turn instinctively to the past for evidence that what they seek has already been found practicable in some former age; and there was no other way when the view of life was universally static. In those days men required documentary authority for their revolutions as well as for their traditions; and they found it, towards the end of the Middle Ages, in the literature of antiquity, in the classics of Rome and in the Bible; and then in the classics of Greece and the Greek Testament, which produced the New Learning, coincident with the invention of the printing-press.

There were both paganizing and Judaizing extremists, but the Intellectual Revolution, in its Humanist as well as in its Protestant forms, was a revolt of Churchmen against mediæval theology, against the monastic orders and the rank and file of conservative clergy.

All this needs emphasizing, because it has long been assumed that art arose, as it were, on the ashes of the

CHRISTIANITY AND ART

Church, and was the result of a pagan reaction against Christianity. A hundred years ago it was thought that even architecture had failed to exist between the Colosseum and Palladio. Symonds, as we have seen, said the same thing about figure representation; and the error is still assumed among those painters and connoisseurs who have had too little historical training. It is important, therefore, to make it clear (1) That a great art existed before the improvements in technique inaugurated by Giotto. (2) That these improvements had no more to do with paganism than had Byzantine or Romanesque architecture. (3) That when the worship of the past helped to produce the Free Renaissance architecture of Florence, in the fifteenth century, it had but little influence on sculpture, and hardly any at all on painting. (4) That Christendom had never broken with the classical tradition but had added elements from Christian Asia and had developed it, Byzantine art being a development of Hellenistic art, and the architecture of Western Christendom a similar development, vitalized also by influences from the Christian East. (5) That the greatest humanists were also good Christians, and that the Intellectual Revolution was a movement within the Church which enormously helped forward her true self-realization, and brought that religion which is common to modern Christendom a good deal nearer to the teaching of Christ than it had been in the Middle Ages.

At first the Church—the Church of the clergy—was torn by conflicting emotions, and in Italy was sometimes pagan and persecuting at the same time—as was Pope Alexander VI, to take an extreme instance. In the end, she failed to adapt herself to the new ideas. Already separated from the Church of the East, the Western

Church—the whole company of Christians this side of the Adriatic and of Russia—was split into a multitude of sects, and so it remains—divided, but not less Christian than it was before the first great separation of the eleventh century. Division has proved to be an unhappy but inevitable stage in the slow evolution of the Church towards the ideal of the Kingdom of Heaven.

Protestantism arose, to modify but not to destroy the art of Christendom. One of the results of the Reformation was that the Dutch masters were induced to divert their energies to landscape and *genre*; and for all this, as for mythology and for portraiture, there is precedent, curiously enough, in the earliest Christian painting—that of the Catacombs. But we must not forget that Protestantism gave us also one of the greatest of all religious painters—Rembrandt.

Iconography is not the determining factor of religion in art, for art is religious in the spirit and not by the letter. Chaucer did not become a pagan because he wrote "Palamon and Arcite," nor Shakespeare, nor Dryden, nor Browning because they, in their turn, made use of mythology; nor did G. F. Watts cease to be a Christian when he painted the Minotaur. The best men among the Italian painters of the Culmination, like Botticelli, Christianized pagan themes, just as the worst have succeeded in paganizing Christian themes.

"Frankly pagan" is an epithet sometimes applied to great artists like Titian and Giorgione in their mythological subjects; but this is precisely what they were not. No pagan Venus was ever like the Venus of Titian: he does not accept her frankly, as one might accept a sister or a mother; he is interested in her because she is so completely foreign to his own ideals of womanhood.

CHRISTIANITY AND ART

His Bacchus, in the National Gallery, does seem to express his ideal of youth : but then his Bacchus is a figure that might in a quieter mood assist without impropriety at an Entombment. Nor are the glorious creatures of Giorgione less further removed from the naïve simplicity of pagan art : their physical beauty is like nothing antique. They are the heirs of Mediæval Venice and of Florence, and the inspiration of many Christian centuries breathes on their unsullied brows.

In modern times the true Church, which is as large as Christendom, has not narrowed her art, but has retained mythology, and landscape and portraiture among the subject-matter of European painting, considering that nothing human can be alien to her : and she has not been the less Christian for that.

At the same time it must be remembered that there had been a good side to the comparatively restricted range of subjects in the Middle Ages. The iconography was indeed not nearly so limited as people imagine ; it included Aristotle and Plato, the Arts and Sciences, Nature, and the most free and varied grotesque : and it is hardly fair to say, as a great living art-critic does, that the Church patronized art " for its own purposes." [1] It was the people as well as the clergy who wanted religious subjects ; it was the ordinary layman who paid the artist, quite as much as the ecclesiastic ; and surely the patronage of the plutocrat has been no improvement on that of the parish church. Artists have to be paid by someone : they have always had to suffer from patrons, and it may be questioned whether the modern period has brought a change for the better. They were sometimes

[1] Bernhard Berensen, *Venetian Painters of the Renaissance*, 3rd edition, p. 9.

overworked in saints and prophets, and were unduly restricted to the Madonna; but at the present day there must be some painters who sigh for the freedom of that earlier servitude, wishing sometimes that they had to paint Our Lady instead of My Lord, saints instead of satin, and prophets instead of profiteers.

The Theory of Resuscitation

To understand the greatness of the Christian developments of art during the settlement of Europe between the years 1000 and 1500, we must discard the misleading talk about the Renaissance which was still unquestioned thirty years ago, and still distorts the views of most writers about art at the present day. Although it used to be assumed that there was no art worth mentioning till the fifteenth century—and very little then—one or two earlier Italian sculptors and painters were admitted by our fathers (more enlightened than our grandfathers) to be efficient, and were therefore promptly appropriated into the Renaissance of some two centuries later—as in J. Addington Symonds' *The Renaissance.* Yet none the less, all artists, good or bad, who had the misfortune to die before Raphael were lumped together in a queer archaic limbo as " Primitives."

Now there never has been a Renaissance or Resuscitation in human history: the idea belongs to a static view of life which has passed away. The world develops by slow or swift stages, with occasional culminating eras, which we call revolutions, but without a break; and attempts at reviving the past do but ruffle the surface of human society: forgotten principles may be recovered,

CHRISTIANITY AND ART

but they can only be applied in the new ways. The utmost we can do for the word " Renaissance " is to apply it in architecture (which rejoices in misnomers) to that recovery from the passing Italian debasement of Gothic which was initiated by Brunellesco in a beautiful mixture of Byzantine and Romanesque, and was afterwards perverted by the discovery and worship of the antique Vitruvius.[1]

There was no Renaissance in sculpture. Hellenistic sculpture had, as we have seen, never ceased, and was the educator of the West. By the twelfth century French masons were already producing that cathedral statuary which is as fine as the best of Greece, as fine as that of Italy in the fifteenth century. It is probably futile to compare together the great exemplars of any art; but now that we are getting over our obsessions about classical perfection and the Renaissance, and are beginning to use our eyes, it is being increasingly recognized that only the finest Greek sculpture, and no Greco-Roman sculpture at all, can be put in the same rank as that of Chartres or Reims, of Giovanni Pisano, or Donatello, or Michelangelo. And if we want to discover one effect of Christianity upon art we can see it in this sculpture. The range is much wider, much freer, and more varied than that of Greece; the types are not less universal, as is sometimes said, but less abstract, and more human; and the faces, instead of being conventional frames of physical beauty, are the expression of every phase of character, thought and emotion, wrought out by the great Florentines of the fifteenth century with incredible subtleness and

[1] There is nothing in Brunellesco's work which he could not have got from the little basilica of the Apostles and the Baptistery in Florence and from the Cathedral of Pisa. If he went to Rome as a youth, as is stated by the unreliable Vasari, his work shows no traces of the visit.

profundity. They were helped, of course, by Greco-Roman examples; but all through the Christian era all the arts had been building upon Greece and upon Rome. Christianity did not invent art; it only improved art. There was no break, except those interruptions in the West caused by the barbarians. And there was no Renaissance.

Modern writers, indeed, abound in admissions, sometimes unconscious, of the fact that there was no Renaissance, though they have not yet faced up to the consequences of their admissions. For instance, Salomon Reinach in his excellent *Apollo* (significant name for a history of art) says: " L'art plastique et pictorale de la Renaissance ne doit pas s'expliquer par l'imitation des monuments antiques. Il y eut en Italie, comme dans le nord et l'est de la France, une première Renaissance au XIVe siècle, qui ne s'inspira pas ou s'inspira très peu de l'antiquité."

In painting also there was no Renaissance. Painting, as we have seen, had flourished through the Middle Ages —that is, from Romulus Augustulus to the Discovery of America; and though most of the fresco work was long ago destroyed or painted over, modern discoveries are steadily filling the gap which was once supposed to exist between Ravenna and Assisi—filling it sometimes with splendid examples, such as those at S. Clemente in Rome.

Painting, indeed, from the thirteenth century has always been Gothic. It had no Vitruvius, and there was no rediscovered Pompeii to deflect the minds of Quattrocento artists: it has gone on developing its fine Gothic realism ever since, and though a Poynter may try to be classical, a Picasso is as obstinately Gothic as ever. There

CHRISTIANITY AND ART

has been the same glorious striving, the same mastery in failure, the same diffidence in success; the same restless pursuit of new methods, the same loyal impatience with tradition, the same sense of eternal youth. And as the discovery of new methods prevails—Giotto, Masaccio, the Van Eycks, the Venetians, the Spaniards, the Dutch, Rembrandt, Constable, Manet, Cézanne—painting becomes easier for us moderns to appreciate, but the actual æsthetic quality is not necessarily therefore increased; and though it is more difficult for people to see into the earlier work, because of what intervenes, it is probable that the sixth-century mosaics of Ravenna, the twelfth- and fourteenth-century mosaics of Sicily and Constantinople, the eleventh-century frescoes at S. Clemente, the mosaics and frescoes of Cavallini, and the Rucellai Madonna (now restored to Cimabue), are as beautiful as even the finest of later work. Is no credit to be given to Christianity for the architecture, sculpture, and painting, and the music also, which it inspired—not to mention a hundred exquisite minor arts which it developed also in its own way? Beautiful though art has been all over the world—for God has never left himself without witness—there is no parallel to the painting of Christendom except in the exquisite but comparatively limited art of China; little to its sculpture outside the Greece of a short period; little among all the beautiful buildings of the world to the breadth and richness, the content, of its architecture; and no parallel of any kind to its music.

Let anyone alter this statement according to any personal predilections of his own—let him, for instance, prefer the trabeated architecture of Greece, with its childlike perfection in limitation, to Durham or Amiens —let him worship the Venus of Melos, or detest all

THE NECESSITY OF ART

painting before Whistler, let him be ignorant of all poetry from Dante to Tennyson—the fact would still remain that to accuse Christianity of being inimical to art is in the last degree absurd, because Christendom has produced the greatest volume of the greatest art in human history.

THE MODERN PERIOD

We have discarded the word Renaissance (except as a convenient though ill-founded architectural term, like Gothic) because it is unscientific in principle, untrue in fact, and the main cause of our mistakes when we theorize about art. The fact that the Mediæval system broke up remains of course unchallenged : it was already rocking in those centuries which are commonly regarded as peculiarly mediæval, the thirteenth and fourteenth, so that if the current use of the term were defensible we should have to include Gothic architecture in the Renaissance. The rise of the guilds and free cities, the disintegration of feudalism and degeneration of monasticism, the growth of criticism, the Humanist development, and the New Learning, the final submergence of Byzantine civilization, the birth of natural science, the revolt of Protestantism, the forming of new centralized states, and the discovery of the New World, all were stages in the transition from Mediæval to Modern conditions. In fact, as soon as Western Europe settled down in the eleventh century, it began to move forward in a changed direction, increasing in momentum till the crisis of the fifteenth and sixteenth centuries. Every stage is illustrated in art, and it would be easy to reproduce the whole story in a series of photographs. Art indeed has its own history, but it illustrates also the whole history of the world, both the

CHRISTIANITY AND ART

spiritual and material, because the spiritual cannot be separated from the material; and art is enormously affected by the political and religious conditions of the people. The weighty civilization of ancient Egypt produced one form of art; the brilliant lucidity of the Greeks another: both were inspired by their religion, both were limited by slavery. Not less characteristic is the overloaded art of Hindu pantheism and caste, or the reforming grace which spread into India from Persia, or the unstable emotionalism of the Arabs and Turks—if the Turks can be said to have any art of their own at all. We might continue: but for our purpose here it is sufficient to point out that the Intellectual Revolution which culminated in the sixteenth century deeply affected art in at least three different ways :—

1. By freeing it from ecclesiastical influences, and thus indefinitely extending its scope. This resulted sometimes in neo-paganism—in the pomps of much sixteenth-century art, or the vanities of the wig-and-patches period; but it also produced intensely religious painting, like that of Tintoret at one extreme and Rembrandt at the other. The old ecclesiastical influence had narrowed Christianity down to a much smaller thing than the religion of Christ, and the adequate expression of Christianity by the arts will probably come about in an era that we have not yet reached. It has been said indeed [1] with some truth that religious painting came to an end after the seventeenth century, and that artists thereupon, being without a subject that could adequately inspire them, took to landscape painting. There has of course been an enormous number of religious pictures

---

[1] *E.g.* by Professor della Seta, *Religione e arte figurata*.

THE NECESSITY OF ART

since; but it is probably true that a great development of real religious art lies before us in the future.

2. The Intellectual Revolution affected art adversely by drawing men's minds to other forms of activity in exploration and commerce, in invention and manufacture, in politics, literature, philosophy, and above all in the ever-increasing forms of science. Born scientists in fifteenth-century Florence, like Uccello or Leonardo, had to become artists, because there was no other adequate means of expression : at the present day a large number of born artists become merchants, engineers, or scientists, because the demand for such services is much less precarious than the demand for art : it requires, for instance, a man of almost saintly qualities to throw up a career as electrician, manufacturer, or stockbroker, in order that he may devote his life to making beautiful furniture for a society that spends its money on antiques. Even within the realm of art itself, the old dominant arts have been weakened by the enormous rivalry since the sixteenth century of the drama and of music.

There should be nothing disconcerting in all this. Man cannot advance both feet at once; and even the tragic litter of the nineteenth century should not blind us to what it achieved in poetry, in science, and in moral progress. The worst horrors are over; art is recovering already, and Philistinism is ceasing to be a characteristic of the educated classes.

3. The Intellectual Revolution wounded art in a deeper way : by its pedantries and its policies it made art an appanage of the rich, and it made people think of art as " a sort of luxurious fringe of life," which the *Encyclopædia Britannica* says that it is. That art has been gradually drained out of the life of the people, and has ceased

CHRISTIANITY AND ART

to be vernacular, is an undoubted fact, however we may account for it. Socialists, guildsmen, mediævalists, Catholics, machinery-haters, draw different veins of inspiration from the past, and not without some elements of reason; though they generally manufacture their own history, and sometimes forget that we cannot resuscitate the past. Certainly art had once been a common enthusiasm; certainly the ordinary village masons and carpenters of the later Middle Ages were able to produce, and seldom failed to produce, works of art that are at once our inspiration and our despair. The change must be largely due to social and political causes, and it is not confined to countries that accepted the Reformation. The Church had once been more the Church of the people; in all countries she passed more under royal and aristocratic influence. Her buildings had been great centres of art for rich and poor alike—not mere picture-galleries or museums, but centres of a living drama which was, in Professor Letheby's words: "the ceremonial life of a people"; they ceased to be this, in Catholic as well as in Protestant countries, though, of course, with a difference, and art passed into the houses of princes and of merchant princes. The causes lay further back than the ecclesiastical controversies; they lay in the intellectual upheaval which affected religion and politics and the whole order of society: as a result of the new knowledge, the quickened intellectual activity, the discoveries and inventions, rich men became more powerful, and poor men lost something which they had formerly possessed. Leaving controversial matters on one side, we can assert that at least they lost their art, both the understanding of beauty and the power of creating it. The very advances in the technique of painting contributed to this; and still more did the learned antiquarianism of Renaissance architecture (and of the Gothic " revival " also) remove art from the common people, and prevent the initiation of the humble craftsman.

Now art cannot greatly flourish unless it is rooted in the life of the people and stimulated by a general demand. A few men of genius will struggle to the top; but art in general will decline, when it becomes the plaything of a small class, and will suffer most in its fundamental forms, in architecture, and in furniture and costume, which are the arts of common life. Such has been the history of the last three centuries, reaching its nadir perhaps, in the year of the Great Exhibition of 1851. Religion and art had suffered together, because together they became separated from the common life of the people; and Europe passed into the age from which we now seem to be slowly emerging, an age (on its bad side) of civilized barbarism, of narrow materialism, expressing itself in dingy sentimentality and flashy shams, an age during which the good word " vulgar " acquired a new meaning.

By contrast with this, the religion of the preceding Christian centuries had been the consistent comrade of art, its upholder and inspirer, with triumphant results; and the life of that art was so strong that it was able to survive both the age of the dilettante and the Industrial Revolution. The very art of painting in its vigorous survival, as we know it to-day, was perfected in the later Middle Ages, and its great masters in that culmination which is called the Renaissance were the children of the Middle Ages, and the inheritors of a tradition which stretched back to the mosaics of Constantine and Justinian and beyond. Those were not more the ages of faith than our own, nor was art then

CHRISTIANITY AND ART

or at any time the meek handmaid of religion; but Christianity had given common men a new sense of values, and of their own value; and they expressed themselves all over Europe, from Byzantium to Britain, in a great art that was distinctively Christian, not so much because it was largely concerned with those popular homes which we call churches, as because, for the first time in history, it was the art of a whole people.

It was this very belief in the eternal value of the individual soul, undeniably a Christian belief, which, as it slowly matured, created the Humanist reaction against ecclesiastical restrictions. In Humanism men at least realized themselves fully as individuals. They broke away —and with the spread of education ever increasing numbers, in Catholic, Eastern Orthodox, and Protestant countries alike, continue to break away—from ecclesiastical domination, nor will they ever return. The Churches first taught them to realize themselves as individuals, and the Churches will have to learn what they taught. Meanwhile there is chaos. The settlement has not yet come: and the effect of the struggle upon art has been to stimulate the painter as an individual, but to weaken the æsthetic sense in the general population, and almost to destroy the arts of common life.

GENERAL CHARACTERISTICS

This Christian art has some characteristics which most people recognize, the free and exuberant variety of its ornament, for instance, its naturalism, inventiveness, delicacy, romance, its aspiring intellect, and genius for progress and invention. The art of Christendom indeed teems with beautiful inventions, like interior space composition in architecture, or the great spandrelled dome, or the spire, or stained glass, or oil-painting as we have it. Every one of its styles of architecture is a marvel of originality; and they owe their very existence to the new religion which first admitted the slave into fellowship and then knocked off his fetters.

So far from Christianity having made art harsh or emaciated, it introduced both tenderness and laughter. It made the very stones to chuckle, and if its great cathedrals seem the embodiment of prayer, they are also like homes where the laughter of children is never far away. In its statuary and painting there is a depth of humanity which the pagan art of Europe had not known; and smiling figures are so rarely found elsewhere that the smile may be included among the characteristics of Christian art, as well as the ability to portray every phase of noble thought and emotion. From this intimate study of the soul of man came all the developments of portrait painting. And was there not also a discovery of the soul of Nature, such as the modern poets have expressed, which built up the later art of landscape? Only in the entirely separate art of China is there any parallel to these characteristics: and China also, as we have said, had a religious principle in its art.

We do not know much about the use of colour among the ancients, except that it was simple and gay. White cities, with here and there a gleam of gold, a bar of red, and a splash of blue—the columns sometimes coloured yellow, as in the Parthenon, to soften the glare of the sun on the white marble—a population draped beautifully in predominant white—such is the general impression we receive. Pompeii shows no signs of development. The invention of colour in Europe as a great æsthetic instrument seems not to be earlier than Byzantine art, and to have achieved its first unqualified success in the mosaics. Since then, colour has become like a new kind of music, a new means of human speech, which we have now in assured possession.

In making such estimates as these, one is in constant danger of seeming to belittle the work of men's hands in earlier ages or under other civilizations. It is not to disparage their noble beauty that I put forward these suggestions, but to show that in Christendom something has been added to art—something indescribably precious. An enhanced skill and science indeed, an extended field of expression, and many inventions, but also a transcendental power—the sense that a man's reach must exceed his grasp, and that all beauty has an eternal meaning; and besides this, a love of natural and human things, not a mere selection of types, as in classical art, but an understanding of ordinary people—of publicans and sinners, of the lilies, and the grass, and the sparrows, which seems to be the mind of Christ himself. Christianity has enlarged both the divine and the human content of art, and has led men—

> "To a land of love and peace,
> Of beauty unknown.
> The world that earth-born man,
> By evil undismay'd,
> Out of the breath of God
> Hath for his heaven made.
>
> Where all his dreams soe'er
> Of holy things and fair
> In splendour are upgrown,
> Which thro' the toilsome years
> Martyrs and faithful seers
> And poets with holy tears
> Of hope have sown."[1]

[1] Robert Bridges, *A Song of Darkness and Light*.

III
THE ART OF MOVEMENT

III

THE ART OF MOVEMENT

By A. S. Duncan-Jones

Vita Hominis Visio Dei.

Man is so made that he responds automatically to that which he sees well done. He finds a pleasure in it, and this pleasure may be mere amusement, just pastime and no more. But lurking within there is a deeper apprehension, a sense of rightness, a cognizance of beauty, and of this the pastime level is a degradation. For if that which is good is approved, it loses its character when the action done is valued just for the titillation of the nerves of the beholder. It must be valued for its own sake. The satisfaction which he feels should not be primarily subjective. It must have about it an element of the absolute and the transcendent. It must be a satisfaction that the thing can be so, or be done so.

Man has then this immediate sense of good, and the only name we can give to it is beauty,—

> "An instinct call it, a blind sense;
> A happy, genial influence,
> Coming one knows not how, nor whence
> Nor whither going."

But when this vision dawns on man, it arouses in him a desire not only to approve, but to respond. He has the immediate sense of a Vision, which something within urges him to translate into action. He must express the value that he feels.

THE NECESSITY OF ART

And this admiration will take one of three forms, or any combination of them which is possible to him whose admiration is kindled.

Let us note in passing that this expression does not follow inevitably. He may just see and enjoy. This is what we mean by amusement or pastime. It is the land of dreams, the country of pleasant idleness, the lotus isle. And most men linger here, and their sense of beauty curdles and becomes corrupt, for it breeds nothing except disease and languor and monotony. If the thing seen is to be the starting-point for higher visions, it must become concrete, it must find expression. In the seeing of the Vision the seer will be quiescent, the whole being is absorbed in the act of sight. But Phœbus must harness his car and grasp his reins firmly and set forth to the daily conquest of darkness. We must be still that we may know God. But we must respond to him, if we would grow in the knowledge and retain the heavenly companionship. The seer must then endeavour to respond to the beauty that he has seen, if his Vision is not to dissipate into dream. He must yield his response. He must make an address. And this address will take as we have said one or more of three forms.

The three forms are :—

Imitation, Imagination, and Applause.

It is not easy to put these in a logical order, but we may try them this way on. A trivial example will illustrate the point.

(1) A good pass on the football field, or a hit to the boundary, produces, at any rate in the young, a desire to go and do likewise. The sight of a thing well done arouses a desire for emulation. And this applies throughout the whole range of the beautiful. There is a beauty

THE ART OF MOVEMENT

in a good life. The revelation of God himself, when it flashes on man as a thing eminently desirable, stimulates to imitation. Man seeks to be like God, even if with fear and trembling. He would fain live the life that he would approve.

His Vision finds its expression in the realm of conduct. There is an art of living. In this art he seems to discern the natural and first response to the Vision he has seen. " What does the Lord require of thee, but to do justice, and to shew mercy, and to walk humbly with thy God ? " Many would say, as Micah seems to say, that this was not only the first but the only true and necessary response. This feeling was to a great extent increased by the Christian experience. God is so great, so the thought ran, that he has never been truly expressed but once, and that is in the Incarnation in Jesus. After that the only thing that we should aim at is reproductions of the Incarnation. Reincarnations in conduct are the only address that man can present to his maker. All else is blasphemy, or at least trifling.

But is it so ? " Conduct " is not the whole of life. It does not cover the whole of man's activity. This activity includes the tendency there is in man to represent in material form the beauty he has seen. He strives to embody the Vision in an image. So we come to the second form of the response.

(2) Man will respond by imagination. His expression of the Vision will take shape in things that are the products of his hand's cunning. He will make temples, and paintings, and sculpture.

Those who have laid stress on the supreme importance of conduct have tended to look with suspicion on this activity. It has no obvious bearing on conduct in the narrow sense. Skill in this line may even be accompanied by an indifference to the demands of the moral law as this shapes itself in the mind of the moralist. In extreme cases this suspicion will be confirmed by a belief that the object of plastic art is to minister to man's pleasure. Thus it may be both a delusion and a snare.

But underneath this attitude there lurk two fallacies : (1) That pleasure is of the nature of sin ; (2) that the object of art is to give pleasure—and pleasure in the lower sense of amusement or pastime. Let it suffice here to say dogmatically (1) that pleasure is not of itself of the nature of sin ; and (2) that the object of art is not to give pleasure, but to interpret in sensible form the truth and beauty that has been seen. But this faculty of artistic creation in plastic form is individual and comparatively rare.

Over and above these individual reactions there is also a desire to give corporate expression to the beauty seen. Man longs to utter not only to others but with others the address that rises to his lips.

(3) At its lowest this takes the form of the instinctive reaction of Applause.

Applause is perhaps the first reaction. It is certainly one of the most natural and universal. Analysed it means that the sight of the beautiful thing excites us to physical response in rhythmic action. Wagner said that if a great audience had taken the last four Symphonies of Beethoven to its heart without alloy it should respond with song and dance. The forms the reaction may take are of incredible variety, from the clapped hands which welcome the smart goal, or the waving of handkerchiefs which acclaim the brilliant fiddler, to the accolade that honours the doughty knight, and the handing of the medal

THE ART OF MOVEMENT

to the saviour of human life or to the promoter of human knowledge.

It is plain to us that this response comes up sharply to recognize human achievement. We feel the rightness of the spectacular acknowledgment; a letter through the post is inadequate to the situation; an element of pageantry is more and more clearly perceived to be a part of social living. What is harder for us to-day to see is that the truth holds good of our relation to God as much as of our fellowship with our neighbour.

And that is perhaps, because we think of God as an absent, static concept. He is our reason for being good as the giver of laws whom we most truly obey when we forget him.

But not so did man conceive him from the first He revealed himself in sacred spot and potent action. He made the winds his messengers, and his ministers were the flaming fires. He caused the streams to run, the seas to boil, and the trees to grow. He was a God who did things. And heaven and earth and all that is therein reflected the awful beauty of his unresting activity. He did things, and he expected man to do things too, to do things which were the response to his operations and the human imitation or applause which broke spontaneously from the bodies no less than the minds of his creatures.

Man instinctively responds to God by ritual. He is dramatic in his religious self-expression. He breaks out into cheers and pæans and psalms. But he also by nature makes his address to God in the rhythmical movement and sacred dance. David danced before the Ark. The gods of ancient Greece not only presided at the dances of their followers, they were themselves dancers. And

THE NECESSITY OF ART

this was not confined to Apollo or Aphrodite; Zeus, Hera, and Athene appear in the character of choragos.

From these things come on the one hand poetry and music, and on the other sacrifice and rite. These at once image the beauty of God, and by their due performance prevent the Vision from turning into day-dreams, and also establish a closer communication with the Vision itself. They enrich the religious life.

We hear it often said that the origin of sacred dance is to be found in fear, rather than in exultation, and is magic and not religion. It is of course true that many of those early ceremonies are " aversion rites "; their purpose is to secure the absence, rather than the presence of the deity. It is true, too, that there is in religion as opposed to philosophy always a certain element of fear. And yet there is always in religious fear something that is not mere panic.

Surely Mr Marett is right when he says :—

> "Of all English words Awe is, I think, the one that expresses the fundamental Religious feeling most nearly. Awe is not the same thing as funk. *Primus in orbe deos fecit timor* is only true if we admit Wonder, Admiration, Interest, Respect, even Love, perhaps, to be, no less than Fear essential constituents of this elemental mood." [1]

The sense of mysterious powers and their relation, whether for weal or woe, to humankind finds its first expression in bodily movement. The procession and the dance are man's first way of externalizing his feelings on such matters. And these movements are not just wild chaotic gestures; but from the first they have definite meaning. They either symbolize some special emotion or set of emotions, or more commonly they

[1] *Threshold of Religion*, p. 13.

THE ART OF MOVEMENT

imitate some act done by worshipful beings. In either case there is an element of acting. They are actions re-done or pre-done; that is the point to note. It is always representation. And here we see the link between art and religion. This it is which justifies us in speaking of ceremonial as an attempt to externalize the Vision seen. The ceremonialist, like the painter or the sculptor, is not motived by a desire to deceive. He is not trying merely to make-believe. His object is to re-live an experience and to re-live it with the heightened emotion which comes from a clear vision of the "light that never was on sea or land." He re-makes ideally. And so it is that rite, and dance, and drama have a common origin, and are in fact at birth one and the same thing. In Sanskrit there is but one word for all—*urtya;* for drama was dance, and dance always presupposed the presence of the gods.

It is when we turn to the fountain of European civilization that we see how closely this development of rhythmic action was allied at once with a sense of sacredness and a feeling for beauty.

The Greek drama is born of solemn ritual and dance. Whether Miss Harrison is right in ascribing the origin of tragedy to Dionysian worship, or Sir William Ridgeway in finding its source in the heroes' funeral rites, in whose honour solemn games were enacted, the main point is clear—drama is dance and dance is worship.

It was so even in comedy, despite its slur of salacity.[1] It sprang from the Dithyramb, the birth-song of Dionysus. For this was never a solo, but a chorus, the song of a band of people, a song needing measured move-

---

[1] "In the Dionysiac theatre there sat to watch the play not only magistrates and priests and eminent foreigners, but also Dionysus himself."

ment, reflecting at once its mystery and its solemn gaiety. It combined the exultation in bodily processes with the vision of unseen powers. You can feel the appropriate action as much as the appropriate music behind the hymn of the Bacchæ :—

> " Achelöus roaming daughter
> Holy Dirce, virgin water,
> Bathed he not of old in thee,
> The Babe of God, the Mystery ?
> When from out the fire immortal,
> To himself his God did take him ;
> To his own flesh, and bespake him ;
> ' Enter now life's second portal,
> Motherless Mystery ; lo, I break
> Mine own body for thy sake,
> Then of the Twofold Door and seal thee
> Mine, O Bromius '—thus he spake—
> And to this thy land reveal thee." [1]

A primitive form of the same truth is seen in the ear-shattering processions of the Chinese. The rattling of drums, clashing of cymbals and thundering of gongs which we are told resound throughout that country every day are a barbaric form of the same reaction, however hard it may be for us to see that mere noise-making can be a form of art, even though as De Groot says, it is gratuitously performed by benevolent people to promote the public weal.[2]

The instinct which prompted a ritual response to God did not disappear with the advent of Christianity. It is true that there are profound modifications—changes in character and quality. " Aversion-rites " do not seem to have formed a part of the early Christian practices. They were at home with God. They knew he loved

---

[1] J. T. Sheppard, *Greek Tragedy*, p. 20.
[2] *Religion of the Chinese*, p. 39.

them; and their love to him was daily tested in a bitter school. Assurance, blitheness, praise, thanksgiving, these are the notes of the worship of the first three centuries.

But the essential thing is there. The rite of the Christians differs from that of the heathen in that it is unbloody. A rite it is, however, nay more, a sacrifice.

Professor Burkitt has well shown this central fact :—

> "Sacrifice was the normal form of everyone's worship, just as prayers and singing is now. New religions at the present day, whatever their principles, tend to adopt a singularly uniform cultus. From what I have heard of the Christian Scientists their meetings are indistinguishable in general form from that of ordinary Protestant worship, viz. hymns and prayers and a sermon. I doubt if people in the early days of Christianity would have been satisfied with that. They wanted something more than philosophy and a frame of mind: they wanted action, something done. So while ordinary folk had their sacrifices, the Christians also had their sacred meal called the Eucharist."

The Eucharist was the Christians' substitute for other people's sacrifices. It was in fact a rite something like a sacrifice. And it has to be observed that this rite seems, as soon as we have clear information about it, to possess a certain elaboration and splendour. The high estimation in which the early Christians held the Eucharist ensured this. They were not Protestants. And so we find a large number of clergy required for the due observance of the sacred rite.

The noble basilicas, which have been elsewhere described, lent themselves to a great corporate act. And it was not only a corporate act: it was a co-operative act. The deacon had the Gospel to read, the subdeacon the Epistle, while the presbyters, who encircled the altar, joined with the bishop in the work of consecration. Other assistants carried vessels and torches and incense.

THE NECESSITY OF ART

The musical part of the service has been compared to an oratorio, for it was distributed among so many different individuals and groups of people. Most of the early evidence comes from the East, but in Rome already in the third century the clergy in attendance on the bishop numbered over a hundred, including seven deacons, seven subdeacons and forty-two acolytes.

But if the Christians of those days were not Protestants, neither were they " Catholics " in the sense in which that word is used to-day. They had a feeling for solemn, splendid, corporate, co-operative worship. And though it had not degenerated into a code, the general scheme was clearly marked. That was ensured by the universal conception of its meaning and reference. But within that outline there was great freedom both as to the words the leader would use, and the exact ceremonial to be followed. They still knew sufficiently what they were doing and why they were doing it to be flexible and elastic in their methods. They had not fallen victims to the Church musician nor to the mind of the sacristan. Bishop Ullathorne was quite in the ancient fashion when, having sat through an elaborate creed till the limit of endurance was reached, he rose in his place, as the choir were singing " genitum non factum " for the eighth or ninth time, and carolled forth : " Factum vel non factum, Dominus vobiscum."

In fact they were not conventional. Their action was still natural expression. It retained its dramatic element. It had not lost all affinity with the sacred dance.

The shades of the law descended upon the ceremonies of the Church. But for many hundreds of years there was still room for peculiarities and local character. The

THE ART OF MOVEMENT

richness of variety was not surrendered without many struggles. It was not till the Counter-Reformation and the Council of Trent, that stereotype which is the mark of Rome to-day, got its grip firmly on to every detail of practice. The ancient Eastern Churches, though they have staggered under blighting political influences too, would seem never to have succumbed to the spirit of law quite to the same extent.

But whether in East or West, and however deadened, or maimed or codified, wherever the Mass has been, there at any rate has been preserved some memory of the great primitive human notion that man's attitude to unseen realities was not merely passive. They were not something he was talked to about. They were not simply something he thought about, nor even a subject of song, though in that a more active element appears. They were something in relation to which he rose up and did something. The intuition of the unseen provokes immediate expression and not merely consequential action. Worship is an earlier response than morals.

The unseen realities, too, kindle a common and co-operative response. They cannot be adequately met by individual activity. They are essentially a thing for the orchestra, the troupe, the band of singers and dancers. The point to be noticed in connexion with the ritual observances, which it has been maintained are man's most immediate reaction to his awareness of supernatural forces, is this: They are essentially corporate, social acts. They are things done by the group. They are emotion socialized. This it is which gives them their great strength, and makes them in their turn the most powerful persuaders to primitive man of the reality of deity. Something which you feel in common with a number of others comes with overwhelming force. It is not only the emotional impact of the crowd that works upon the individual; it is also the enormous power exercised by public acts customarily done, and received by the community. So it is that men will continue ceremonial observance through fear of society or lingering affection even after the import of the thing done has long lost its grip on their minds.

But the question may naturally arise : " Is the dance a form of art which man's need for expression will always require, or is it only a phase ? "

It is one which cannot be properly answered without a somewhat long digression.

Music and Religion

But rhythmic action is indissolubly wedded to rhythmic sound. The sacred dance involved an accompaniment of music. At first this was probably merely an accompaniment. But in that accompaniment there lay concealed a giant, who for centuries was struggling to the birth. The history of music is the record of an often baffled striving for autonomy. But it is also a record of doubt and hesitation, as to whether when that freedom has been achieved, the real purpose of music has been discovered. Is music a maiden, finding her perfection in virginity ? Or is she more properly a being destined for the married state, one who finds in union her true function and fruitfulness ? Is she in danger of losing her bearings, when she wanders far from drama, dance and song ? When form rather than matter becomes the sole object, is not the white beauty of virginity in danger of becoming the mere dullness of sterility ? Anyhow the impetus to sheer music, to

THE ART OF MOVEMENT

beautiful sound, as an absolute form of expression would not be restrained.

The Church melodies are a clear example of the struggle. The Church naturally set a high value on the sacred text because it was of an origin indubitably divine. Adorn it, by all means (so ran her mind) but adornment must be with restraint : it must not distract from the main issue. However, the musician would have his way, even in Church, where he could. The Alleluyas of the Middle Ages and the bravura of Handel are witnesses to the impulse of the musician towards untrammelled expression, even in the Liturgy.

Whether such expression is justified and to what extent is a matter for discussion. There is from an artistic point of view much to be said for the enforced decorum of the Church. For absolute expression is only satisfactory, when it comes from a personality at once sufficiently strong and sincere to have something worth expressing. A Byrd or a Mozart is justified by his children; but a Meyerbeer or even a Puccini becomes intolerable when he attempts more than decoration.

The whole question of absolute music and its place in the domain of beauty is of extreme importance to anyone who is investigating the common roots of art and religion. For there can be no question that historically not only has all religious ceremony employed rhythmical sound, but the development of music has also been a product of Christianity.

In the first place Christianity revived music. Greek music was sinking or indeed had sunk into degradation. The impulse was exhausted, when the Church provided a new one. The materials, the scales, were the same. So was the melodic range and the points of repose in the

THE NECESSITY OF ART

scale. What Christianity supplied was a new motive, and by a happy accident a new race, and that one the Italian, in whom music was latent, but undeveloped. The genius of the new religion brought new points to the surface. Mainly these were a greater simplicity and breadth. The Greek aimed at individual interpretation of the text. The Christian at the communal expression of adoration in the utterance of sacred words by great multitudes. The sense of solemnity was aimed at, but at the same time a breadth of feeling which would incorporate the devotion of the whole congregation.

The flowing melodies of "*Deus creator omnium*," or "*Vexilla regis*," or "*Pange lingua*," are the unhindered expression of a new vision of truth and beauty. They move with a sustained enthusiasm. They reflect the gladness of a company of people who have moved out of darkness into light, and are at once exhilarated and awed by their discovery and their deliverance.

The new impulse which Christianity gave to music did not soon exhaust itself. The "Dark Ages" witnessed a steady growth and development which endowed the Church with perhaps the largest body of pure melody that has ever existed. And more—busy minds devoted themselves to the study of the principles that underlay it and to the evolution of its science.

The ignorance of the cultivated world with regard to all this is wellnigh complete. *The Cambridge Mediæval History* in its first volume has a chapter on Early Christian Art in which this most signal achievement of the Christian spirit is not mentioned. In the second volume it manages in one place to couple the word "music" with the name of Gregory. In the third volume the subject is waved aside with an apologetic gesture. "No idea of the

THE ART OF MOVEMENT

progress made in Music can be given, but by a specialist." As the specialist was apparently not forthcoming, we are left to console ourselves with the reflection that the shadowy and sordid history of emperors, counts, and viscounts was at any rate relieved by gorgeous buildings and learned writers.

The musical impulse renewed itself again and again, finding as each new age appeared a fresh source of inspiration in the Christian Mythos and the Christian Rite. The popular Sequences of the later Middle Age were succeeded by the glories of the great polyphonists. After that, it is difficult not to feel that a subtle change passes over the music which professes to derive from religious themes. But their spell persists. Purcell, Handel, Bach, Haydn, Mozart, Beethoven, Verdi, Wagner, Elgar. In this list not all are equally great, nor are their " Christian " works necessarily their greatest, or in the truest sense their most religious. And yet the *Messiah*, the *Passions-musik*, the Mass in D, *Parsifal*, the *Apostles*— these do not only represent an attempt to meet a popular demand. They are not simply made for hire. Especially is this true of the *Requiem* of Mozart. We remember the picture of the broken genius worn to a shadow by the stupendous theme, bursting into tears as he reached the words :—

> " Lacrimosa dies illa
> Qua resurgat ex favilla
> Judicandus homo reus.
> Huic ergo parce, Deus."

It shows how this greatest perhaps of all the magicians of sound, flamingly hating the chicanery of the Church, yet responded to the epic which was the Church's supremest treasure, as to a thing which could command the soul of man.

THE NECESSITY OF ART

What is the reason for such failure as there is in the great works to which allusion has been made ? It is a subject worthy of close study and detailed analysis. Two suggestions only may be hazarded. The Renaissance and all that has flowed therefrom broke up the mental universe, and ever since there has been a sense of strain in man's outlook on the deepest things. It is probably true that these three hundred years are the germination of a new and greater unity. But meanwhile the mind is in pain.

There is another reason of a different order. This was the time when music was struggling to secure its own autonomy. It could no longer be the handmaid of the Church ; nor did it wish to be merely an appendage to the drama. Even lyrical song would not satisfy it. It was fighting through to quartet and symphony and tone-poem.

And yet it is true to say of the whole development, as does Wagner, that " the only music, which, now, at least, we can place on the same footing as the other arts, is an exclusive product of Christianity." Christianity, not Islam or Buddhism or Hinduism, has, as a matter of fact, supplied the atmosphere in which music has come to its maturity, if indeed it has done so yet, and is not rather a very young art still. We can say this, while fully recognizing what Mr Fox-Strangways says about the wealth of Indian melody.

So great has been the achievement of music that it might fairly be claimed that it is the art of the modern world. Music has become for large numbers of people the one form of expression which they feel answers to their deepest intuitions. It is the thing which comes nearest to the religious activity. It is that one of the

THE ART OF MOVEMENT

arts in which great work is most intelligently appreciated by the technically untrained mind. Large audiences applaud not only Beethoven, but also Richard Strauss or Stravinsky with enthusiasm and sincerity. They would be hard put to it to analyse or explain what they heard. But it is improbable that they would be so moved by any statue or picture. They would agree with Wagner again, not only when he says that strictly speaking the only art that fully corresponds with Christian belief is music, but also in his utterance touching the Sistine Madonna: " That sublimely virginal Mother of God lifts us up above the miracle's irrationality only by making it appear as wellnigh possible. Here we have: 'That signifies.' But Music says: 'That is '—for she stops all strife between reason and feeling, and that by a tone-shape completely removed from the world of appearances, not to be compared with anything physical, but usurping our heart as by an act of Grace."

And yet it may be doubted whether this is not a phase.

DRAMA, DANCE AND RITUAL

Wagner's ideal was a whole where scene and song and poem and instrument blended into the exhibition of one great idea. There are limits beyond which music cannot move except at its peril. It can do many things absolutely without alliance or assistance; but, as has already been observed, rhythm and melody lie at its roots, and divorced from them it will wither. Moreover it is an applied art. It may stop the strife between reason and feeling, not by ministering to the direct Vision, but by providing an excuse for day-dreams and

THE NECESSITY OF ART

pastime. Indefiniteness, haziness are not the marks of beauty. May we not say that mere listening will not satisfy the soul of man, any more than will mere seeing? Surely it is in such a work as *The Magic Flute* that we see the supreme achievement of music. There is content as well as suggestion, matter worked out in form. There is indeed a place for reason in art, since art cannot afford to be either mere emotion or mathematics. The image is essential to art, but its value lies in its really imaging, and in its having something real to portray.

In the drama we get this: but for the fullness of the drama music is needed, and so is the dance. It is in the delicate interweaving of poetic words and rhythmic action and musical form that the great truths which " in manhood darkly join " can best be symbolized. For it must be remembered that it is symbol we are in search of—true symbols, adequate symbols. It is the making of symbols, and the reading of them, which constitutes the life of man. When they are achieved and recognized we know that through that life there shines the light of God. It is then our soul leaps up and we are glad.

" Complete contentment," said Schopenhauer, " the truly acceptable state, never present themselves to us but in an image, in the work of art, in the Poem, in Music. From which one might surely derive the confidence that somewhere they exist in sooth."

The dance then in the largest sense will persist. For it is only in the combination of the arts which make up the perfect drama that the soul of man can be most perfectly liberated.

But it will only persist in so far as men are possessed with great truths which they are burning to express. History shows that the play and the ballet, more than any other form of expression, degenerate speedily into banality when they are divorced from a sense of ultimate values. There must be a motive of a transcendent kind, if the theatre is not to be mere pastime. There is a place for diversion in the theatre. But the rule even of its salvation is expression, not imitation. Even when it is diverting it must express, if it is not to fall.

It is an interesting fact that a long course of drawing-room comedies and problem plays in realistic surroundings left not only the great mass of men untouched, but also provoked a reaction in those who demand from the drama a complete expression of the human spirit. Their realism was not rich enough for reality. *The Second Mrs Tanqueray,* and *You Never Can Tell,* were all the time performed against a background of musical comedy and revue. When the Russian ballet of Diaghilev came upon the scene, it was hailed as the liberation of hidden forces, which had for long been denied a voice. The revival of Mozart's operas, which have leapt so suddenly into a firm place in popular esteem, has been due to the realization that in them you had the imagination of a genius working freely on big truths passionately held, and finding its expression in action and movement. Into the most trivial story he breathed a large-hearted sense of the dignity and lovableness of man. There is a faith behind. "We are groping for faith," Mr St John Ervine has said; "and when we have got some sort of religion then we shall get great drama." The drama, we may be sure, will always find men hungry for it, as long as it is based on conviction and faith. And the more it seeks to bring into the lives of men the great truths, not because it wishes to teach, but because it is itself possessed by them, the more it will find its perpetual justification; and the

THE NECESSITY OF ART

more it is possessed by these truths, the more it will try to draw the spectator into its life by a combination of all arts of movement, colour and sound.

"To draw the spectator in"—that is the secret. Strictly there should be no spectators. All must be actors. But the conditions of the modern theatre are delicately constructed so as to keep the spectator outside as far as possible, to prevent him from ever getting lost in what is going on, to remind him that he is just putting in the time between dinner and bed. The greatest dramas of the world, the Greeks and Shakespeare, were all constructed and performed so as to concentrate on the essential, spiritual problems. And their method of performance was designed to unite in a spiritual unity performers and audience. Only those who have played Shakespeare in a small room with the actors right in the middle of the audience can have any idea how closely he grips.

And there is another reason why the drama is of enormous value. It is not only because it provides the most effective means of opening the eyes of the generality of men to the world of ultimate values, but even more because it is the art in which they can take the most personal part. Pictures and music for most of us are merely to be seen and heard. But nearly all people can act, especially if they begin young. Art is doing. To take part in one Shakespeare play is of more value to the average man than many picture galleries. If the young actors are encouraged to express not themselves but the great poet through the medium of themselves, they will have discovered something about God, which they never could have learnt any other way.

If it is true that through the drama we can so well

express our sense of ultimate values, the last question that comes up can the more easily be answered. Is Ceremonial an integral part of religion? Or is it just the baby language of faith, which we must and ought to leave behind? For hundreds of years there have been those who would answer at once that rite and ceremony were things which man had outgrown, or should outgrow. Some of the Hebrew prophets would be among their number, though, as Dr Oesterley reminds us in *The Sacred Dance*, it is a mistake to suppose that belief in such things was confined to those who come first in the history, only to be abandoned by the giants of a later day. It was not only Saul and his barbaric contemporaries who practized the ecstatic dance. Dr Oesterley marshals evidence which shows how widespread was the sacred dance, confirming what has been said above as to the instinctive nature of ritual, while at the same time it illustrates how thin is the line which separates ceremony from dance. A procession is in effect a dance. It is an expression in action of an attitude towards ultimate reality.

When we are considering the survival value of such reactions, it is well to remember that they were of a higher and a lower order. In the latter we may class rites, which have for their object the compelling of the god to do the will of his worshippers, to bless the crops or provide game. The aim of this type of dance is the procuring of some material benefit. But there were higher thoughts behind many of these ceremonial actions, thoughts of proclaiming and recognizing the majesty of the deity, thoughts of union with ultimate reality, thoughts of communion with the departed. Granted that amongst primitive uncultivated people these thoughts

THE NECESSITY OF ART

would often find crude, childish expression, have we any ground for supposing that all such thoughts are to be forbidden, when man desires to respond to that which he has seen of the beyond? Are quietism and contemplation the only forms of religious expression? It would at any rate be possible to argue that where such ideas had prevailed, the religious sense for many ordinary people, no less than for many of strong artistic feeling, had become atrophied. A corporate and universal religion can hardly be built on the ideal of the hermit. Communal aspiration demands public expression, and the instinct for pageantry lies deep in the human breast. If frowned on by religion, it finds an outlet in other ways. The Lord Mayor's Show is a poor substitute for the pilgrimages and processions of the Church. The dumb instinctive ceremonial of the Cenotaph is a warning that something stirs in the human heart, which we have by our conventions too long made men forget.

If we could put away prejudice, and foster healthy impulses, we should find that the modern man, because he still is man, would be glad to release his need for expressive action, and to embody in appropriate performance his sense not only of sex (as at present), but of the good, the beautiful, and the true. He would pay in drama, drama which included both song and dance, his meed of applause.

It is worth remembering that the Christian idea of God is itself imaged in the form of a great Drama. A divine action on the human stage shows us what God is and what he has done for us. Historically it would seem that it is the recognition of this that God has done that has been the nerve of the Christian religion. It has been differently phrased at different times, and expressed in

THE ART OF MOVEMENT

terms of different philosophies. But behind all beauty of teaching, and beyond all marvellous deeds, there stood the great fact of the Divine Being who voluntarily offered himself as a sacrifice, and in so doing effected over the mysterious powers of evil a conquest in which his followers could share. This was the affirmation to which the Christian was to make his response. Is it to be wondered at if he " rose to " it ? Does it not naturally suggest an immediate " applause " ? It is then only in line with what we might expect that we find embedded in the tradition a rite like the Eucharist, which, as we have seen, is of the nature of a drama, a way of reliving that which God had done for the worshipper. And it is a drama which naturally gathers round it music and symbolic action, and thus lends itself to the assistance of a whole company of graded ministrants, each with their part to play. But it really insists on the co-operation of all. It does not forbid spectators. But it quite clearly is designed to make them " actors." And when the other parts of religion lose their appeal, when men find it difficult to place faith in the sacred writings, or to accept the formulas or creeds, yet this action will retain its attraction and seem filled with a reasonable, serene, and lofty mystery. Certain it is that many to whom prayer is always hard, and who are as far as possible removed from the *dévot*, have found in assisting at the altar a new sense of the unseen beauty, and a confidence that they are making an appropriate response.

IV
THE PURITAN OBJECTION TO ART

IV

THE PURITAN OBJECTION TO ART

By Malcolm Spencer

I. The Puritan Attitude

An historical treatment of the Puritan movements in religion which have from time to time put forth a philosophy of life either negligent of art or antagonistic to it, would be a long one; for religion has constantly shown a divided mind toward the artistic side of life. On the one hand, religion has used art freely in its service. On the other hand, it has feared art as a trickster or a rival, a delusion or a snare. Indeed, the higher the development of religion, the more has this attitude of mingled fear and condemnation shown itself. It is the more ethical and spiritual religions which have produced the Puritan movements of history, and they have done so because of their ethical and spiritual emphasis.

Thus it was the intensity of the Jews' realization of the greatness of God that made them fear to express his being in any image, or name his name in words. The impulse which drove the Eremites into the desert in the early days of Christianity, and which created the monastic life of the Middle Ages, was an impulse springing from the higher elements in Christianity—from its hunger for fellowship with God himself and for holiness in his service. So, too, the Puritan movement of the Elizabethan and Stuart period in our own history was animated by ideals great in themselves and congruous with the very highest conceptions of life and religion.

The men who created these movements went out from the world as they knew it, because they really did see the vision of a better and a truer. Their sense of God's greatness and man's dignity made the life around them seem mean and petty, unsatisfying to their craving for a life of absolute value. They were repelled by the triviality of the life of the courts and market-places, the temples and theatres of their day. They were afraid of the contamination of the higher susceptibilities of those who occupied themselves with these superficial and seductive activities. And they sought refuge in flight. They forsook the world, with its compromises and temptations to vanity and selfishness; or staying in the world they took hold of its carnal pleasures and its religious observances and stripped them of the elaborations and excrescences with which they had overloaded their appeal to sense.

What we are concerned with, however, is not so much the history of Puritanism as with the general attitude to life which it reveals alike in the Puritanism of the past and in the Puritanism of the present day. Our interest is not archæological but psychological. We desire to bring out the Puritan attitude to life and confront it with the non-Puritan attitude. And we can do this without any elaborate historical analysis; for the Puritan is in every dozen human beings, if not in every single one. And the non-Puritan is as universal. May we then with no wish to docket and label the complex movements in which Puritanism has expressed itself in the past, define the Puritan attitude in this way ? The Puritan is a man who is afraid of a sensuous and superficial reading of the

THE PURITAN OBJECTION TO ART

universe. He is afraid of forfeiting the inward to the outward, afraid of losing God in the enjoyment of God's creation. His love of that which is beyond the world makes him distrust the manifold riches and colour of the world, and fear the attempt to use them to the full. The attitude is essentially one of flight, and of negation; a fear of enjoyment because of the seductions of enjoyment. The Puritan, it has been said, practized a mechanical process of salvation by refusal, and was full of malice against those who were saved without refusal.

II. THE TRUTH OF THE PURITAN PROTEST

Now the Puritan attitude may be open to criticism, but it cannot be lightly dismissed as merely perverse or uncultivated, much less malicious. It springs from a high ideal of life, a profound reflection upon good and evil. Puritanism attacks the lesser values in the interest of the values that are paramount. It does so for the sake of those spiritual realities which are the ultimate aim of art as well as of religion. If it errs, it is in a noble quarrel, and it is not without sound argument, though the argument be incomplete.

The Puritan is right in two, at least, of his main contentions. He is right to insist upon the illusion which lurks in all attempts to represent the highest in sense forms, and he is right to insist upon the snare which may lie in every form of sense satisfaction.

Take first the limitations of the attempt to represent by any art, in any medium, all that the spirit knows of its own glory. It is impossible so to express the soul in bodily form that the form infallibly conveys the spiritual idea which was the artist's meaning. That probably is

THE NECESSITY OF ART

the root and the truth of the Puritan suspicion of art. The artist looks for the spiritual reality which another artist has expressed in matter: he is taught to perceive it and he does. But it is not there inevitably and unmistakably in the material medium. It is only there for those who have eyes to see. And for those who have not,— who miss the spiritual meaning of a picture or a poem or a drama or a dance,—there are other meanings to intrigue the mind. The danger is that the sense appeal of the artist's work will overwhelm its spiritual appeal. It may even be that the sense appeal of the material has already drowned the soul of the artist before ever his work was given birth. His music, or his portraiture, may express the vision of a man who has been captivated by the external glamour of life, who has missed the soul of the thing he sought to represent and bodied forth an enchanting vision of the superficial or the second best. There is in every work of art, as there is in every life or action, the appeal of its blemishes to the baseness of the beholder. To the Puritan the danger of artistic misrepresentation outweighs the possible value of the power of art to suggest the good and the true.

For those who live easily and superficially, this peril of misrepresentation will seem slight. But it cannot be so for the true Puritan who has tasted of the moral splendour of life and peered into those abysses of sensuality into which man is so easily betrayed. He is on fire for the pure gold of experience, and most of all for purity of religious experience. No wonder then if, when art has attempted to depict his own most ineffable religious apprehensions and experiences he has sometimes recoiled from its ineptitudes and turned from it in dismay. Art of the second best, attempting to portray the spiritual

THE PURITAN OBJECTION TO ART

realities known to the most sensitive of religious souls, may well account for such repulsion.

For though art may express, it may also hide the truth: it can belittle and distort the idea it would embody: it may even kill the soul of truth. Indeed for the unwary, religious art must always do one or other of these things. The most high God could not express his love to man by anything less than his incarnation. No other representation of God's nature can be more than a shadow and symbol of that unique manifestation in the forms of human life. If that is remembered, well. But if it is not remembered, as the Puritan thinks that it is always liable not to be remembered, religious art is a seducer. In point of fact the Puritan movements of history have not usually occurred unless this danger of seduction has been real and imminent. They are the outcome of periods when art has been debased or misapplied: when it has been degraded to the service of lust and voluptuousness, as was the case with the drama in the day of the Roman Empire; or when it has been too closely bound up with false conceptions of deity, as in the days when Judaism proscribed the further use of the arts of sculpture which Israel had acquired in an idolatrous environment.

We pass to a second point at which the Puritan plants himself on the bed-rock of truth. He sees that art may be made a substitute for life. Instead of being content to play its part as the interpreter, it may aspire to adopt the rôle of life itself. It may make its appeal to the enjoyment of the senses the end of all effort and desire. It may offer man beauty and rhythm and sweetness, as things to pursue for their own sakes—and as things attainable on their own terms, and in a domain of their

THE NECESSITY OF ART

own—instead of portraying these things as qualities of a larger life containing other ingredients and tuned to other ends.

Art, as Goethe said, should be man's comrade, not his guide. As a guide, art is too little sensitive to man's moral goal. "Art," says Forsyth, "is often careless of the moral foundations of life. It can even cast a glamour about evil and make sin doubly engaging." But then so, too, may religion.

As beauty may be a siren to lure man to his destruction, so, too, may knowledge, if it be not controlled by an ideal inclusive of all life's values : and, though the Puritan fails to see it, even morality is, in this respect, in the same boat with beauty and knowledge. Unless they are in harmony, any one of them may draw life out of its proper course. As knowledge may pervert, so morality may choke the spirit of man if it sets up to be itself alone the arbiter of man's life and the sum of all life's values. We shall return to this point later in the argument. Meantime we note that the Puritan has often shown himself susceptible and even notably susceptible to the artistic appeal, when art has been properly harmonious with his life purpose. Indeed at such times Puritanism has been the parent of great art, as when the Cistercian Puritans gave mediæval architecture a fresh inspiration and when Luther in Germany and the Calvinists led by Bourgeois and Goudimel in Switzerland, loosened the bands of music and gave to the Northern races a fresh opportunity of free and popular expression in religious song. So, too, some of our greatest literature is due to the Puritanism of the Hebrew Prophets, whilst it is chiefly within a Puritan environment that we find the cult of gardens raised to the level of a fine art.

THE PURITAN OBJECTION TO ART

III. THE PURITAN ATTITUDE CRITICIZED

Turning from appreciation to criticism, it will be well to deal with an assumption which underlies the Puritan objection to the arts of representation as applied to religion, the assumption that you can do without them. The truth is that if you are going to share your vision with your brother, you are bound to employ the arts of representation and incur the inherent danger. There is not a choice between art and no art : there is only a choice between art untrammelled and art in chains, between art in colour and art in monochrome. The Puritan in religion reduces the art of representation to the art of speech, not recognizing that speech is as much a form of art as any other mode of representation. He may even admit the art of song, as he does in religious worship, provided it is brought in decorously and with due subjection to the merely spoken word in homily or sermon.

It is, however, a mistake to suppose that language is anything else than an art of symbolic representation when it touches religion. We misinterpret the function of language, and miscalculate its limitations, if we suppose that language can convey any more infallibly or unmistakably than music or painting the precise meaning and value of a religious truth. Language, like any other form of representation, can only suggest the truth by picture and analogy. Very often it is the poetic beauty of a phrase, even more than its value as an instrument of definition, that makes it able to convey a vision of God or of goodness. There is a scientific sphere in which language may be quite precise, and there is an element in the expression of religious truth in which the relative precision of language over other forms of artistic representation plays its peculiar part. But its very precision is limitation and mutilation of the truth, if we fail to allow for it. It is indeed this failure to understand the limitations of verbal definition which accounts for half the misunderstanding between Catholic and Protestant, Traditionalist and Free Churchman.

In support of the assertion that you cannot escape from dependence upon art by fleeing from it, witness the Nemesis which befell the Jews' attempt to avoid the representation of God by any image or by any word. They reduced the name of God to an algebraic symbol and they crystallized the idea of God into a code of rules. Apart from the dramatic ritual of the Temple and the dramatic poetry of their Scriptures this was the tendency of their Puritanism. Witness again the naïve inconsistencies into which the Puritan is betrayed. He slips so easily from prose to poetry and from poetry to song. Music having found entrance into worship as an accompaniment to singing, wins presently a place in its own right. Architectural effects are sought with surreptitious explanations. Pictorial designs invade the windows of the churches which have driven them from their walls. Thus time plays havoc with the vain hope of avoiding religious error by avoiding religious art. And the more art is eschewed as mischievous, the more mischievous is the effect of such art as is in fact allowed. When art is banished as a serious ally of religious representation, it returns as a mischievous sprite to adorn our religious services with mere decoration in colour, with meaningless prettiness in architectural design, with banal emotion in rhetorical gesture and speech. Or, if it be eschewed entirely, dullness and ugliness creep into the untenanted

THE PURITAN OBJECTION TO ART

emptiness and twine their suggestions of negation round our unconscious conceptions of God.

Mere negation cannot protect and dignify the truth. The negation of beauty in worship is not a final protection against sensuousness. It is an unfortunate establishment of the lie that God is indifferent to the beauty to which he has given being. So to despise the warmth and colour of life as to divorce them from the worship of God is to blaspheme his glory and in the long run devitalize the nature of those who permit the blasphemy. The Puritan fear of gaiety and colour in the worship of God and in the precincts of his temple has led to a parody upon God's character. It has associated the thought of God with repression, and placed lightheartedness under the ban of religious disapproval. To the Puritans who set the world on this track of æsthetic death no such mere negations were conceivable: their thought of the moral splendour of God made up for the deficiencies of their æsthetic presentation of him. And so it is still wherever the sense of that moral splendour is uppermost: the warmth and joy of life are expressed in other terms, but that fact cannot destroy the subtle tendency of Puritan practices to teach the separation of art from life, religion from beauty, sense from spirit. Against all such teaching Nature, in the end, has her revenge. She entraps the Puritan into the indulgence of his desire for sense satisfaction in some unregarded matter —the Puritan is by no means always an ascetic in food and drink—and she turns the natural human instinct for sense delight into repulsion from a too restricted religious appeal.

We are now back at the point from which we set out in criticism. The Puritan has found the splendour of

THE NECESSITY OF ART

God too exclusively in the realm of man's moral struggle —his struggle for the purification of his will. He has been obsessed with the difficulty of being good and avoiding evil. He has made his own bad conscience too much the pivot of his philosophy. The evil bias of the human will is indeed a big factor in life. Man's tendency to choose evil rather than good and his need of divine help to deliver him: these must ever be largely determining elements in the philosophy of any man who has been made acutely aware of them. But human conduct does not fill the universe and its consideration should not monopolize man's consciousness. The self-conscious will, with its freedom and its enslavements, is not everything, though it is so much. God is not fully expressed in man's deliverance from evil humours and degeneracies. He has made honour and beauty and instinctive virtue as well, and the free spirit responding joyously to the call of abounding life.

It is bathos to suppose God concerned only with the problem of our behaviour, and that chiefly under the temptations to selfish excess. He has surely set us on a larger stage in a world whose meaning may centre for us but cannot be exhausted in the problem of our faithfulness to the recognized duties of our religious and social life. But such in effect is the Puritan narrowing of the issues of life. It gives value only to the conflict in which the savage and the egoist in man contends with the claims of God and of his fellows. It does no sufficient justice to the richness of that ample life to which it is his privilege to gain entrance. Concentrating upon the sector of human life in which the self-conscious will is the dominant factor, it banishes art *ex hypothesi* from the realm of real value. For art is by definition concerned

THE PURITAN OBJECTION TO ART

with an expression of the human spirit with which the will has no direct concern. As Schopenhauer has defined it: "In the act of æsthetic perception the will has absolutely no place in consciousness."[1] The intelligence is then for a while released from serving the practical ends of life, in order that it may abandon itself wholly to the perception of things in themselves and apart from their possible use. And from such moments of pure contemplation it comes back to the world of action refreshed and invigorated. In the long run morality is not the loser by these excursions. The human will works best when it has learned to ease the strain of uninterrupted exertion. As the new psychology is fully proving, there are laws of reversed action which paralyse the will that is never unbent. The will is in reality under the domination of the imagination,[2] and in the long run a man's conduct will be good according to the range and beauty of the things which he admires.

IV. CONSTRUCTIVE

And here we can begin to correlate appreciation with criticism and speak constructively, dealing first with the principle that life is more than conduct, and that God has more functions whereby to excite our worship than the function of helping us to be good. If we narrow life too strictly to conduct, we impoverish conduct, because we starve imagination. Conduct then tends to become narrowly utilitarian. This may surprise the Puritan, whose desire to refer man's conduct wholly to God, and make man concentrate his energies entirely upon obedience to the divine will, would seem to lead only to

[1] *The Metaphysics of Fine Art.*   [2] As Coué says.

THE NECESSITY OF ART

the ennoblement of conduct and certainly not to its impoverishment. But the charge is true none the less. The nature that is not constantly reinvigorated by fresh perceptions of the goodness and beauty inherent in things becomes in its material activities an unconscious slave to the sin of ministering only to the more animal needs of itself and others. The fear of being ensnared in self-indulgence leads to a paralysis of the power to enrich and benefit other lives. For a man's power to inspire and help his fellows depends in the end upon the wealth and variety of his capacities for enjoying himself. If he is himself indifferent to the manifold delights of living, he will presently come to restrict his services to his fellows to the limited gamut of his own powers of appreciation.

The historical proof of this is found in the type of civilization issuing after some centuries from the great stimulus which the forces focused in the period of the Reformation gave to man's constructive and organizing energies. The result has been to prostitute the physical energies of mankind mainly to utilitarian production, with but the very slightest regard for beauty or grace or any other thing than the satisfaction of man's mere bodily needs. This miscarriage must not of course be put down simply and crudely to the defects of Protestant theology. More likely it was due to the general defects of the thought of the time. There was no adequate philosophy of æsthetic which the religious man could fall back upon. Naturally, the Reformation thinkers, in their preoccupation with the moral issues in religion, failed to do justice to the æsthetic issues, and the religious and moral defects of the æsthetic activities of their day confirmed them in this disregard of the fundamental

THE PURITAN OBJECTION TO ART

importance of a right æsthetic. It was not that they despised art or were insensitive to it. Calvin, for example, if one may trust his Dutch exponent Kuyper, places the æsthetic planes of man's experience above the intellectual and ethical planes. Through art man is mystically reminded of the beauty of God's ultimate design for the universe.

It is perhaps the very closeness of art to religion, in history and in idea, that makes Calvin distinguish between them and make them appear as rivals. But though art is thus belauded by him in theory, it is belittled in practice, and so the lack of any truly religious philosophy of æsthetic in the thought of the Reformation period fixed modern Christendom in a mood unfavourable to the recognition of beauty and its place in life. It thus reintroduced into Christian thinking an opposition between flesh and spirit, soul and sense, alien to its principle and foreign to its past. The religion of the Incarnation had resolved that opposition, as the art record of the past millennium properly proved. The sixteenth century reinstated it. It allowed the tides of human energy that it quickened toward material achievement to flow apart from the tides of spiritual energy. It made an idol of Utility and set it up in the market-place to be worshipped there as God. But when men cease to look for God in the beauty of the world and find him too exclusively in the qualities of human diligence, obedience, and self-control, they sacrifice much of the grace of Christian character, and become hard, ignoble, and in the end cruel.

The idea of Nature as God's medium for revealing himself to man gives the saving salt of spiritual meaning to all kinds of sense activity. We can now eat and drink to the glory of God, not finding his glory chiefly in our own abstemiousness in eating, but chiefly in his bounty in providing:—

> "Nor soul helps flesh more now
> Than flesh helps soul."

Restraint and discipline are brought into play not because sense enjoyment is a snare to be escaped but because it is a sacrament to be shared, a sacrament of God's love to the human family too precious to be defiled by sensuous over-indulgence; a sacrament of family fellowship too enjoyable to be appropriated with selfish greed. The conquest of sense is attained by the spiritual interpretation of sense. And since it is the artist's function to show men, in the things which appeal to their senses, values which should appeal to their souls, the artist and the Puritan are true allies. Are they not both entrusted with the divine gift of interpretation, that is to say, of revelation? Are they not both seeking to find in the temporal, the eternal; in the life of the flesh, the spirit of God? Are they not both seeking the divine meaning of experience: the one through the interpretation of what man does and ought to do; the other through the interpretation of what man perceives or might perceive?

For the Puritan, like the artist, is a man with a vision which demands expression,—only he is unique in his choice of his medium. His medium is simply his own life and behaviour. Ruthlessly he submits to the necessary limitation of his interests and activities that he may give single expression to the thing which he sees in God. He is like the sculptor chiselling away the stone which will not fall within the limits of his design. The

THE PURITAN OBJECTION TO ART

necessities of the design make him, as they make every artist, within limits, an ascetic. With the Puritan, who has but one life to be wrought to the shape of his vision, the restriction is necessarily more ruthless and prolonged than with the artist generally. But this asceticism for the sake of an idea is of the essence of all artistic triumph, and the artist should be able to recognize it in the Puritan. Perhaps, too, the artist can teach the Puritan not to despise the material he cannot weave into his immediate design, as the Puritan tends to do. So long as he only restricts his own immediate and personal use of the facilities which life affords for innocent delight, he is within his rights. It is when he comes to despise and forbid the things he has himself rejected that he oversteps them.

If the Puritan and the artist would recognize their partnership in this business of spiritual interpretation, each might help the other to escape from his particular entanglement. The Puritan might find a way out from the obsession of the problem of his own sin and his deliverance from sin. The artist might realize better on what a nice edge of equilibrium the spirit of man is poised: how prone he is to vanity and the allurements of his lower nature; how often he stands in need of disentanglement; how greatly he needs the master-key to his experience, the knowledge of himself as an eternal spirit evolving in a transitory world of sense forms. Were this partnership effected, the artist would be the ready ally of the Puritan in his passion for austerity in religious art, for severity and reserve in the expression of his religious feeling. Here, if anywhere, man's spiritual expression should be chaste and noble, cognizant of the majestic simplicities of his nature, of the solemnity of his moral choices, of the awful splendour of his spiritual

THE NECESSITY OF ART

deliverance. It is not the artist but the mere furnishers and upholsterers who have been the foes of the true simplicity and purity of Christian worship.

The genuine Puritan and the artist are partners, too, in their need to seek some of the criteria for their craftsmanship outside their own crafts. Art for art's sake, and religion for the sake of religion, are both alike condemned. There is more in life than either art or religion. Life in its full compass alone affords the criteria for our judgments of absolute value. It has been already urged that religion in its concern for the purity of man's conscious volition, may easily conceive too narrowly the ends that are worthy of humanity. Art, on the other hand, needs some principle of selection to regulate its concentration. Not everything is equally worth looking into, and at any given moment in the life of an individual, or a nation, some things are best left alone. Art is for revelation; a medium through which the artist interprets to his fellow his own vision of the divine, and it will depend upon the perceptive capacities of his contemporaries, as well as upon his own faculty, what he is able so to express. Puritan and artist are both alike in an occasional inability to consider what their symbols will mean to their contemporaries and to translate their vision for the understanding of their times.

What then is to provide both art and religion with their ultimate criteria? Surely it is the conception of a universal Brotherhood, in which each individual seeks to perfect the life he has received from the one Father and to put his gift, developed and disciplined, at the disposal of all. The instinct of the artist is to be dominated by his own genius for self-expression. He has more power of original self-expression than his fellows: what more

THE PURITAN OBJECTION TO ART

natural than that he should make his self-expressiveness the single aim of his development? The argument pointing that way is strong, but it is incomplete. The artist, like every other man, is a social being, husband and father it may be, but friend and citizen of the world-commonwealth without exception. He must exercise his gift of seeing in such wise that he is not a negligent husband or father, a fickle friend, or an apathetic citizen. Nay more, he must find in his citizenship the great second principle that is to determine the direction of his art. To his own being and to the God who made him, he owes it to see what he sees with a single eye, and to express what he expresses with absolute sincerity: but to the world-brotherhood he owes it also that the things which he chooses to interpret shall be things that will be for their peace. To fulfil his function in the world he must eschew churlishness and take into account the needs and capacities of those to whom he may be life's interpreter. And if he would be a Christian as well as an artist he will care supremely that his art should express his message not to his own satisfaction merely, nor to the satisfaction of the few elect souls who have been already deeply initiated into the world's spiritual secrets, but to the awakening and satisfying of a like capacity for appreciation in the souls of common men. He will work for the poor and needy—the poor in æsthetic appreciation and the needy in spiritual insight. His aim must be to evoke from the multitude that perfect response to the divine perfection which is his ideal for himself.

V
THE ARTIST AND THE SAINT

V

THE ARTIST AND THE SAINT

By Alfred W. Pollard

FUNDAMENTALLY, the psychology of Science, Religion and Art is all one. We have not three different equipments for these activities, though the methods of using the equipment differ in details. Each of the three activities at its highest is the product of man's leisure, of free meditation and recollection, of the birth of new ideas through the unconscious movement of the spirit, touched, as we believe, by a spirit greater than itself. In each the mind roves over its problems, attains a vision which satisfies, and (if it is wise) proceeds to test and verify this vision, not only in other ways, but in practice, if that be possible, in order to see how it works, and correct and improve the first sketch.

In the reception of the vision the will has no part. The presence of will either distorts vision or nullifies it.

The will is of immense importance, but its special function is the persevering maintenance of the right orientation and the right expectancy, so that the one thing which we can pray for without any fear of a reversed effect is for the union of our will with that of the personal beauty, truth and goodness whom we call God.

THE NECESSITY OF ART

Science, Religion and Art are alike in another respect. In each there are three classes of recipients :—

i. Recipients at first hand—original creators and discerners of laws and forms ;

ii. Recipients at second hand—the assimilators, exponents and popularizers ;

iii. Recipients at third hand—the formalists and imperfectly equipped teachers, who look only to their text-books for what they shall teach.

Alike in Science, Religion and Art the man who carries new visions most completely into practice is not necessarily the first recipient. Inventors die in poverty ; prophets are bad husbands ; the " new artist " often lacks judgment or technical skill. Not always, but often, the new vision is too great for a single human personality to discern and assimilate it in the maximum completeness possible to humanity.

In religion we call the men who come nearest to completeness in carrying out the vision *Saints*. The art of life is to keep our spiritual eyes turned to the divine beauty ; to keep ourselves keyed and tuned to receive it, and to carry out our visions in thought, word and deed. The Saints are those who come nearest to doing this. They differ according to the epochs and the countries in which they live, according to the different lines on which the religion physically possible to them is developing, and the stages which it has reached. But despite these differences there is much family likeness between them.

The man of science, the saint and the artist, are alike in yet another respect ; they are all human beings, with

THE ARTIST AND THE SAINT

human temptations which disturb their orientation and key them to receive other messages than those they are seeking. If they could overcome these temptations and had sufficient breadth of receptivity, there is no reason why one and the same man should not be a saint of science, a saint of religion and a saint of art. If Leonardo da Vinci had been a great Christian and had had an opportunity of showing it, he might now be hailed as all three, though in that case he might have painted different pictures. It is difficult to conceive of such breadth, and yet men have been found willing to make sacrifices alike for science, religion and art; and to be capable of making sacrifices for one should render it easier to make sacrifices for the others. Yet it seems to be a fact that absorption in scientific research lessens susceptibility to art, and absorption in art lessens interest in science. Few human brains are big enough to be eminently susceptible, eminently interested, in both respects.

If it is a fact, as it seems to be, that the human brain is seldom big enough to be eminently susceptible both to science and art, are we to say that the indifference of many men of science and many artists to the technique of religion is due to the human brain being seldom big enough to be eminently susceptible both to religion and science, or both to religion and art? Most of us think of religion primarily as helping us to " be good," though it is also largely thought of as helping us to escape punishment for having failed to be so, which is not the same thing. Half a century ago Matthew Arnold wrote of goodness, " morality," as constituting for most men three-fourths of life. It would, perhaps, be more true to say that the endeavour to be good constitutes three-fourths of our spiritual life, which is mostly itself miser-

THE NECESSITY OF ART

ably dwarfed and attenuated by the pressure of our daily routine, be it our bread-earning job, or the pleasure-seeking to which we turn as a relief from it. Now the spiritual lives of the artist or the man of science, like those of other men, may be dwarfed by their routine; but on the other hand, in so far as they are specially concerned with the pursuit of beauty or truth, they may find themselves predisposed to criticize what is presented to them as religion, on the ground either of the defective psychology with which goodness is pursued or of what seems to them the defective morality of some of the doctrines as to how punishment may be avoided. Art and science do not criticize each other in this way, and we are thus bound to admit that the opposition of science to religion or the opposition of art to religion, where it exists, is at present of a different kind to the complementary opposition of science and art. Science and art challenge Religion, because they see it as ineffective in its primary object of helping men to be good, and as incomplete because it does not teach men to seek truth and beauty. On the other hand, those who value the practice of religion are convinced that to be satisfied with a reverent attitude towards life without common prayer or worship, or any conscious effort at communion with God, ends also in ineffectiveness and incompleteness. Both the challenge and the counter challenge seem pointed and true, and we are obliged to look for a harmony in which Religion will be seen, not only as a rival to science and art, but as a unity in which these are subsumed, along with the pursuit of goodness, so that men's ideals may be less incomplete and less incompletely attained. The groundwork for this unification exists, since already religion may be found by the man of science in his

THE ARTIST AND THE SAINT

science and by the artist in his art, though what they find need not be technical religion (which mostly involves some organized form) and is not necessarily Christian.

As such, art and science can only be in sympathy with any organized form of religion in so far as the organization recognizes their own religious aspects, which many forms of religion deny and ignore. In its largest aspect the whole of religion is that men should glorify God and enjoy him for ever with all their powers and capacities, and if the form of religion professed and practized excludes the worship of God as Truth and Beauty, with which the man of science and the artist are specially concerned, then science and art will be out of touch with that form of religion. There have been varieties of the Christian belief, which have taken very little interest in truth and beauty, and therefore have regarded both science and art as hostile to religion, and have helped to make them so. But to those who believe that God is the Eternal Truth and Beauty, as well as the Eternal Goodness, and that the Kingdom of God which Christ preached is the conforming of our human nature into his, truth and beauty are essential elements in a full Christianity. Yet, while they are essential in this sense, it is not by these that Christianity is differentiated from earlier religions, least of all from the religion of Plato. As set forth by Christ from whom it takes its name Christianity is specifically and distinctively the realization of God as the loving Father of all the human race, and the glorifying him and enjoying him as this, with the necessary corollary that, because God loves all his children, he demands of them all that they shall love one another. When we analyse it, this Christian conception of God

THE NECESSITY OF ART

restores beauty to its primacy, because we are so constituted that we find beauty in those who love us and those we love, and the vision of the love of God is the most beautiful that can come to the human soul. But as with every other revelation that has come to man, so with this revelation also, there came a possibility of misusing it as well as of using it, and in men's concern for their private salvation the vision for centuries was robbed of its power. Broadly speaking, it is only within the last half-century that the envisagement of God as the loving Father of all mankind, and the zeal for the coming of his kingdom, have regained a dominant place in religious experience.

Now Art can only with difficulty transcend the religious atmosphere of its own day. In so far as religion admits art into her sanctuary, art does not fail her. Greek art is instinct with the fortitude, justice and temperance of which Plato wrote; mediæval art speaks of devotion and aspiration; our modern English art of respect for character in fine men and women, of pleasant scenery on sea and land, and of comfortable houses, items not prominent in our Church services, but which bulk largely in the natural religion of well-to-do Englishmen, who (since the Churches ceased to buy pictures) create the demand which artists, if they are to make a living by their art, must satisfy. If the Churches complain, they may be reminded that it is usually the saints that practize the virtues most convenient to authority who are selected for canonization. The saints with inconvenient virtues have more often been burnt. The saints with inconvenient virtues in art are not burned, but they run some risk of starving, whether they are painters, poets or musicians, before they come into their

THE ARTIST AND THE SAINT

own. Nevertheless they stand a better chance of ultimate canonization, and their canonization is more of a reality. The number of the formally canonized saints of religion who make any real appeal to the modern imagination is much smaller than that of the artists. Yet not all of these help us to see the world and our fellows in a new way, and this (as Rembrandt, for instance, effects it) is the true communication of vision.

As already noted, below the little band of true visionaries in art, literature and music, as in religion, are the happy assimilators, the men who can reproduce with their own touches of individuality beautiful forms which they have learned to love and have helped to inspire others to love also. And below these, in each case again, are the men who have been caught young, because of some youthful flashes, which seem to them, or their advisers, the forerunners of the true fire, and who have to stick to their job to the end of their days, however it irks them, because they are fit for none other. Should any man be accepted a priest of religion, or a priest of art unless he has learned some craft on which he can fall back if his capacity for receiving the divine fire fails?

It is said that men have to be set aside for these priesthoods early, before their strength and weakness are known, because art is long, and theology is long, and the necessary technique can only be acquired by the patient study of many years. The answer cannot altogether be gainsaid, but there is room for some division of labour alike in art and religion, and the technique, though it should exceed the minimum required for use, should be in reasonable proportion to this. The cult of technique for its own sake smothers more individuality than it elicits, and the fresh individuality content to address

THE NECESSITY OF ART

itself to elementary tasks is of more help in teaching others to see, than the laboriously acquired learning whose products are often merely dull. The point is of importance, because while those who here prove their special capacities for these priesthoods and ministries in Art, Science and Religion may rightly be set apart as wholetime searchers and exponents, there is a responsibility in this respect on the shoulders of every man who comes into the world. To learn to see, and (in thankfulness for any gift of sight that comes to us) to try to help others to see also, are surely the two things best worth doing, though most of us may fairly be required day by day to do our share of the world's drudgery before we set about them. To seek any one of these ministries, consciously or unconsciously, mainly to escape drudgery, is damnable. It is also doubly unwise, since disinterestedness in the seeker is one of the conditions of the quest, and if common experience may be trusted, it is through the alternation of drudgery cheerfully performed and leisure wisely used that most of us have our best chance of attaining vision.

Science is comparatively free from the special temptations to take it up as a pleasant way of earning a living which beset both art and religion. We need not underrate the drudgery involved in the study of theology and the numerous subjects of which the clergy are now expected to know a little, nor yet the discipline of hand and eyes necessary to make a painter, nor the kindred training needed for other arts, but there is a hard intellectual element in science, testable by examinations, which does not encourage young people to adopt it as a profession with any subconscious hope of having an easier time than their fellows. Yet taken as a whole,

THE ARTIST AND THE SAINT

the professions of helping the world to see goodness, of helping it to see beauty, of helping it to see truth, have much in common, and the professors would all do their work more efficiently if they were more in sympathy with each other. The average man up to a point has a genuine admiration and respect, even a reverence, for all three. He respects their positive achievements; he respects them as examples of the height to which men may attain along the lines of their several developments; he finds them materially useful to him, as specialists mostly are. But in his heart he tends to suspect all but the best of them as shirking their share of the world's drudgery; even the best he suspects, unless their special gifts are combined with a patent and generous humanity, of being something less than men. The first thing which men expect of one another is that they should be true to type, if possible true to a progressive type, but still recognizably alive and whole. The average western man (whom the western professors have to educate and therefore cannot neglect), though he underrates the value of vision, does not despise it; but he has very little respect for the visionary. He reserves his respect, even his tolerance, for the man in whom he can see vision reacting on personality, and the vision-inspired personality finding its expression in life, or in that readiness to lay life down for the sake of a cause which makes a greater appeal than the most eloquent words.

We know something of the average western man historically for some three millenniums, by anthropology for many more. His maximum of physical efficiency and brain power does not seem to have increased during this period; whatever theory of evolution we may adopt, evolution as a subconscious process seems to have done

THE NECESSITY OF ART

for him pretty well all that it can. Throughout this period of history men have found it easier to struggle with each other than with themselves. Throughout this period of history also we see men and women oversexed, tormented by their own pursuit of sexual pleasure apart from the desire for children. The problem of religion has become more and more how to help men to a new orientation, a new attitude towards God and their fellows, by which they can be saved from the perversions of the instincts of self-preservation and reproduction, and so be helped also to climb further along the steep path which leads to man's proper end, the glorifying of God and the enjoyment of him for ever. When, with varying emphasis and differences of interpretation, the ideals of beauty, truth and goodness had been accepted alike by Greek and Hebrew prophets, a definite step forward had been made from which the western mind, the inheritor of both traditions, cannot retreat without moral suicide. Neither as seen and interpreted by Greek nor Hebrew did the vision provide the necessary stimulus to project man on to a new plane; but the ideal became a standard, a trio of tests, by which later on Christian doctrine and practice themselves came inevitably to be judged, as soon as any measure of freedom of thought and expression was attained.

Christian philosophy as we see it in the writings of S. Paul and S. John, did not discard the ideals of beauty, truth and goodness, but transferred its main emphasis to three others which make them personal and dynamic. Beauty, truth and goodness are all in themselves abstract and static, concerned with the vision received or attained, not with the personality which gives itself to or for others. Transmute beauty into Life (Ζωή), transmute truth into Light (φῶς), transmute goodness (or righteousness) into Love (ἀγάπη), and the words become energizing and creative. Ζωή is the life which God has in himself, the life which Christ came that his followers might have and have more abundantly; φῶς is the light which is equated with God himself, so that it can be said " God is Light," and the " Word " the light which lighteth every man that cometh into the world, so that his light, too, may shine on others; ἀγάπη is the love which, like light, can be equated with God himself, so that it can be said " God is Love," the love from which nothing can separate us and which evokes a human love that never fails, and is greater than faith, greater than hope. Life is greater than beauty and yet beauty is its test, its standard, its judge ; light is greater than truth, and yet truth is its test ; love is greater than goodness, greater than righteousness, and yet goodness and righteousness are its tests. The Christian words are the greater ; we can do with nothing less ; but the pre-Christian words, the three which declare to us the ultimate realities, desirable for themselves and for no other reason, are here more than ever needed as tests and standards, because we must be sure that when we see them energized with personality the abstract qualities retain their definition. In the English language 'life' stands both for mere existence and for the life which is worth living, because of its quality, and 'love' both for sexual desire and disinterested affection. Thus these two triplets, the standards and ideals of Beauty, Truth and Goodness, and their embodiments in personality as Life, Light and Love, not only cover the ground of human aspiration, but recall also the physical basis from which it springs, and on the health of which its own progress largely depends.

These remain, indeed, as they always have been, elementary physical tests, which can only be ignored for adequate reasons, and then at a man's peril; though to override them when the adequate reason is present is the admitted proof of fine manhood and womanhood.

All the reality of Religion and Art and Science comes from the interaction of the ideals expressed in these six words. The three we take as our tests, Beauty, Truth and Goodness, must be always challenging each other to make sure that the Beauty is really beautiful, the Truth is really true and the Goodness is really good. If what seems to us beautiful and good is not true, the beauty and the goodness are to be suspected as shams; and if what seems to us true is neither good nor beautiful, we may suspect the truth of being at least incomplete. The three must be harmonized in one, or each ideal is imperfect. So again beauty challenges life to be sure it is worth living; truth challenges light to be sure it is pure; goodness, righteousness, challenges love to be sure it is honest. But these tests must themselves be tested as to whether they are alive, active, generous. Six things taken two at a time yield fifteen combinations, and an old-fashioned preacher might pursue the subject under fifteen heads; and his sermon would exceed the length of the longest ever preached, before he had exhausted the applications. Moreover, alike in religion and science and art, because the subjects are varied and complex, there are aspects which are real as aspects and though they may rightly be challenged, when they seem to have become stereotyped, they may yet rightly be valued. Giotto challenged the Byzantines because their pictures lacked life, and Velasquez challenged the Italians because their pictures lacked truth, and yet the art both of the Byzan-

THE ARTIST AND THE SAINT

tines and the Italians at its best was great art. In religion those who live by the sacraments and those who live by the spirit challenge each other, and yet both may truly find what they rightly seek. Art, science and religion are ever incomplete, imperfect. In religion we believe that God is Beauty and Life, that God is Truth and Light, that God is Goodness and Love, and that because he is all these they are all one and the Trinity in Unity and Unity in Trinity is to be worshipped; but we believe also that we can only realize an infinitesimal fraction of what God is and yet that he accepts any least bit of reality in our worship.

VI
LITERATURE AND RELIGION

VI

LITERATURE AND RELIGION

By J. Middleton Murry

WHAT is Religion ? It is a thing at once so abstract and so intimate, so indefinite and yet so real, that only a personal definition can avail, and even a personal definition cannot be produced at the sound of a trumpet. It needs a preliminary, tentative self-examination, and an endeavour to impose upon shapeless feelings a form against which they may rebel. Nevertheless, we must make a beginning.

Religion, let us say, is the sense in the human soul of a binding relation between itself and God. A definition with two vital and ultimate terms undefined, perhaps indefinable ! For what is the human soul ? And what is God ?

My soul is my self, the ultimate, irreducible I, the dark spring of living water within me on which my life depends, an essence not to be apprehended by my mind, for my mind is only a partial manifestation of it—a living spirit whose nature can be uttered only in the tremendous and mysterious words of Jehovah : I AM THAT I AM. The old falsity of the *Cogito, ergo sum* is far away from us now : for we know, as our minds cannot know, that it is untrue. Not *Cogito, ergo sum* is the mark of the soul, but *Sum, ergo cogito*. My soul is my profound, unutterable

THE NECESSITY OF ART

being, that manifests in thought, in feeling, in act, and above all in life which comprehends all three. My consciousness of my own freedom is my consciousness of my soul.

And what is God ? Shall we say : That greater I AM to which my own I AM acknowledges a binding relation ? The logician will say that we are burking definition. " Read your sentence again now "—he laughs—' Religion is the sense in the human soul of a binding relation between itself and—that to which it has a binding relation.' " And yet, somehow, we are not disturbed. We did not imagine, when we began, that logic would have much help for us. Let it solve the mysteries of its own tremendous problems, let it master the secret of Quanta ; or let it admit that the structure of the universe is non-rational. And if the structure of the macrocosm be non-rational, the structure of the microcosm is assuredly also beyond reason. Beyond reason, without a doubt, is our initial certainty that the living soul exists. Will the logician challenge it in the name of reason ? Whether he challenge it or not, we must go our way ; we must be loyal to our certainties.

Perhaps, precisely because this binding relation of the human soul to that which is beyond it appears to us unequivocally to exist, we can best approach the nature of God, in deliberate independence of the laws of logic, from the immediately apprehended nature of the soul. The point at which the nature of the soul rises nearest to the light of the intellectual day is in our consciousness of the indefeasible freedom of the living self. Without that consciousness, we die ; and if we deny it with our minds, we nevertheless accept it with that which is deeper than our minds, for unless we accept it, there

LITERATURE AND RELIGION

remains to us nothing to deny it with. We *must*, therefore, acknowledge our freedom; and that of which we acknowledge the freedom is our soul.

We begin, then, with this: our immediate apprehension of the soul as the subject of the freedom which we know is ours. And this same immediate apprehension tells us more. Though our consciousness of the freedom of our soul remains unimpaired, there are certain things we cannot do; and these certain things are not such as are forbidden by the nature of the external world, wherein we freely admit necessity, but such as within ourselves we feel at the same moment that we are free to do and bound not to do, or free not to do and bound to do. In theological language, we are confronted with the mystery of conscience; but the word conscience, worn thin, like most theological terms, by centuries of disputation and casuistry, will no longer hold what it must contain. The immediate experience to which, in the language of Christian psychology, the word conscience corresponds, is in itself as much positive as negative. The " Thou shalt " is at least as frequent as the " Thou shalt not."

What we feel in ourselves is this. In the heart of an essential freedom which is ours, which we have called the freedom of the soul, there is a sense of inner obligation to obey the command of something deeper even than the soul itself. Of our souls we are, save in sleep, continually aware; the consciousness of our fundamental freedom never abandons us. But the voice of this inner command is intermittent; it may be silent for days and months together when there remains only the sense of our obligation to obey it when it is audible. Perhaps the inward reality of this experience has never been more truly

THE NECESSITY OF ART

expressed than by the lines of the French poet, Paul Claudel, describing his own religious conversion:—

"J'ai fui partout; partout j'ai retrouvé la loi,
Quelquechose en moi qui soit plus moi-même que moi."

For this voice, when it sounds, sounds to us as the voice of the innermost I; this law is, indeed, more myself than I. And our obedience to it is not an abrogation of our soul's freedom, but a consummation of it. Our consciousness of this command is the deepest point of our knowledge of our own identity. Here we touch the very quick of being, the secret core where self passes into not-self and is born as self once more; this and none other is the meeting-place of the soul and God, the moment of contact and fusion between the I AM that is within and the I AM that is beyond—beyond, because we know it as exceeding the soul's capacity, and apprehend it immediately as infinite. It is the ocean wherein we drown and the fount whence our life springs. And at the point in our exploration of the soul's reality where we see the necessary and living identity of personality and impersonality, we comprehend quite simply the meaning of Christ's mystical saying: "He that loseth his life shall save it," for the essential life of the soul consists in a losing of the soul for its own renewal.

The sense of this inward motion, the consciousness of this binding relation between the two I AMs, is what I understand by the word religion. It may be formulated, I imagine, in a thousand different ways and articulated in a thousand different systems: but the formulation in the sayings of Christ is one, I believe, which can never be superseded. It is simple, naked and essential, and it touches the heart of the mystery more nearly than any formulation of which written record remains to us.

LITERATURE AND RELIGION

If, therefore, as I believe, religion is the fundamental reality of the human soul; if the consciousness of the soul itself demands for its very existence the consciousness of God; if the lesser I AM can only be in virtue of the greater I AM from which it draws its life—then literature, which is a manifestation of that same soul whose deepest anatomy is contained in religion, must inevitably be knit up with, be indissolubly bound to religion. There is no escape. Religion and Literature are branches of the same everlasting root.

No doubt, in so far as each may depart far from its living centre, the indissoluble bond between them may sometimes be hard to discern. The vital motion of religion becomes petrified into dogmas and ceremonies; the vital motion of literature is ossified into forms and canons; and between these empty husks the connexion is invisible and non-existent, precisely because it was a connexion between the living essences. When literature becomes a parlour-game and religion a church-mummery, they are alike only in their deadness. But between the literature that is real and the religion that is real the bond is close and unbreakable.

So close and unbreakable, I could almost believe, that in those periods of human history when religion is at once superbly organized and close to its own living centre, the creative impulse of literature might well be enfeebled because the need it satisfies is less urgent. Perhaps the coincidence of the time when the spiritual and temporal realities of the Christian Church seemed identical and the time when Western literature was moribund is not in the least fortuitous; and it may be that the decay of dogmatic religion, because of its failure to express the religious reality and supply the religious

THE NECESSITY OF ART

needs of the soul, is a necessary condition in order that literature may truly grow and flourish. It may be that the moment comes when the finest and most sensitive minds are compelled to be of the Church but not in it; when, precisely because they are profoundly religious, they are bound to work in complete independence of what passes for religion in their day.

Certain it is that, since the Renaissance, literature and religion in the West seem at the first sight to have gone their separate ways, so that the mere attempt to establish and make visible what seems to some a self-evident connexion between the two realities, appears to others either an endeavour to undermine the foundations of religion or a manifest blasphemy against the sacrosanct conception of " art." Yet, surely, these fears are purblind. One man may surely admit, even while he feels that a systematized belief is necessary, that religion is more than systematized belief; and another may surely admit, even while he feels that " art " is necessary, that literature is something more than " art."

Of course, no man is a writer simply because he has a soul. He needs besides the gift of expression, the faculty of using words creatively so that they compel his readers to think and to feel and to see as he desires them to think and feel and see. And we may, if we choose, completely isolate this faculty from all others with which it may have an organic connexion, and declare that this and this alone constitutes the essence of literature. But this beginning will not take us far; we find, very soon, that by this act of isolation we have killed the living object of our inquiry, having severed it from its root. To consider this maimed and desiccated literature is like trying to apprehend the nature of flowers by contemplating

LITERATURE AND RELIGION

those plucked and rootless blossoms which German children stick in the turf of a grave. They droop and wither while we look at them.

We cannot apprehend a work of literature except as a manifestation of the rhythm of the soul of the man who created it. If we stop short of that, our understanding is incomplete. We may enjoy, we may be thrilled, we may imagine that we are appreciating some absolute of æsthetic perfection; but we are only sensationalists. We cannot know its essence and its individuality. For, if we take this consideration of a work of literature as a thing-in-itself at its highest, as an appreciation of some absolute æsthetic perfection, two imperious obstacles bar the way to a full understanding: first, the fact that æsthetic perfection must be absolute, and that all writings which possess it, considered from this angle, are the same, because there can be no difference in the quality of an absolute perfection; and, second, that in fact hardly one of the works of literature which, by the consensus of generations, are reckoned great, possess this quality of æsthetic perfection. Shakespeare, Tolstoy, Dickens, Dostoyevsky, Keats, Stendhal, Wordsworth, Whitman, Carlyle, Balzac —not one in a hundred of the works of these masters can, by the wildest flight of imagination, be called æsthetically perfect. They have style, they have individuality, they have life; they move us profoundly, disturb and delight us: but to call what we feel an æsthetic emotion, or that in them to which we respond an æsthetic perfection, would be a wanton misuse of language.

The great writer has to be two things. He has to be a writer: to have the gift of compulsive language, of words that live and impose thoughts and feelings upon those who read them. And he has to be great; he must

THE NECESSITY OF ART

have a quality of soul that is profound, and because it is profound, is universal. His soul plunges deeper and soars higher than the fashionable feelings of his day. Conventions of sensibility may fade away, and others come to take their place, but the rhythm of his deep waves is undisturbed by these superficial rufflings. He is a prophet of what is eternal in the human soul.

There is always, at all times and in all places, a shallow literature of convention and fashion, created by superficial sensibilities, for the amusement of those many people who require from an author a reflection of their idle selves and a satisfaction of their trivial appetites. They turn away in fear from the prospect of being made to see unfamiliar sights, or to feel disturbing feelings, or to think thoughts beyond the reaches of their souls, which are hide-bound for lack of exercise. They have a vague presentiment how uncomfortable, how positively catastrophic, it would be if their souls were to be wakened into life, and they avoid the danger as they would the plague—but still more instinctively. A dead soul is bound to shrink from contact with a live one. They want their literature soothing and narcotic and innocuous. "How beautiful," they murmur at their tea-parties, " and what style ! " Yet a glimpse of true beauty would frighten them out of their lives, and an inkling of the real nature of style would send their timorous minds squealing down the road to perdition.

For there is something awful and terrible in the work of a great writer, even though he may be like Dickens or Gogol a master of what is called Comedy, for the Comedy that does not consist in the bandying of airy repartee is based on a savage and ruthless vision into the nakedness of human nature. The comedist laughs, we all laugh;

LITERATURE AND RELIGION

but if we were to stop laughing, something queer might happen. We have to keep Sairey Gamp under control, lest she become a portent, and Tartuffe lest he become a monster. Even Falstaff may develop a trick of growing uncomfortably titanic. And the nearer we approach to the living soul of the great writer, the more are we aware of the immensities between which that life of his is perilously swung. For as we approach the creative centre of his work, we are able to read it, nay we directly experience it, as the record of a struggle for being. His books are the battle-ground of his soul. In them he fights for life and a faith without which life cannot exist, and his struggle is the more terrible, the more moving, and the more profound, because he is by nature aware of so much more than other men. His faith must justify more, just as his life must include more, than the faiths and lives of other men.

And, just because the great writer is an adventurer on behalf of humanity and is, in these latter days at least, the archetype of conscious man, his effort is essentially religious: but essentially, not superficially. We shall not discover much about the bond between literature and religion by hunting through the great writers for sentences that may be used for texts for sermons. The writer is seldom occupied in praising God; his effort is to discover or to rediscover him. An anthology of snippets like

"A robin-redbreast in a cage
Puts all heaven in a rage,"

may be edifying and reassuring, as tending to show that these lawless and incalculable persons are really pillars of the Church. But the fact remains that they are nothing of the kind. They search for God, because they are pre-eminently men, and because it is a law of the living human soul that the connexion must somehow be established. But theirs are perilous adventures, and they do not return from them to the calm safety of a harbour they have left. If they find a harbour, it is a new one, not by any means to be identified with the old. They are not prodigal sons who return, having wasted their substance, to their father; far rather, in their rediscovery of God, do they recreate the reality of religion. Their progress ends not in an abjuration of their error, but in a triumph of their truth.

But this assertion that literature is the record of a soul's struggle after life and God may not appear so necessary and self-evident to my readers as it does to me. "Think of *Tom Jones*," they may say, "or *Pride and Prejudice* or *Alice in Wonderland*—where is the soul-struggle in them?" Well, honestly, I do not believe it is there. There is a soul manifest in Fielding's and Jane Austen's books, otherwise they would not have the strong individuality we recognize in them; but it is not a struggling soul. Nevertheless, if we look at the whole course of Western literature since the Renaissance, we shall find that placid and undisturbed personalities like these are not really characteristic. The great figures of the period are shaped after the pattern of Shakespeare—they are nearly all what is generally called "Romantics." But if we regard Romanticism as an attitude of soul which was unknown before it descended upon Europe in the person of Jean-Jacques Rousseau, or if we think of it parochially as a return to nature and a revolt against convention on the part of a handful of English poets at the beginning of the nineteenth century, we shall never

LITERATURE AND RELIGION

understand either Romanticism or the epoch of consciousness in which we live. Romanticism was something that happened to the European soul after the Renaissance; and the essential fact of the Renaissance was that man asserted his independence of an external spiritual authority. It was a movement of expansion and growth, which became vaguely conscious of itself because of the New Learning. Men, who had long been silently chafing against the restraints of an established and omnipotent religion which by the mere magnitude of its organization had lost contact with the individual soul, gained confidence in their own impulses from the sudden revelation of an epoch before their own. They saw that a time had been when the spirit of free inquiry had flourished, and men like themselves had lived outside the shadow of the terror of death and the life to come. The veil of mist that had obscured the past from them and made them feel that the dispensation under which they lived was established in the very nature of the universe, was suddenly rolled away. They could see what had been; therefore they could see that what was, was not absolute, but relative, not the eternal creation of God, but the temporal handiwork of man.

To gain some inkling of what the Renaissance meant, one has only to remember the lovely and famous lyric of Villon, the enchanting and lonely cry of the bewildered human spirit in the Dark Ages:

> "Dictes moi ou nen quel pays
> Est Flora la belle Romaine
> Archipiada ni Thais
> Qui fust sa cousine germaine?"

For the answer to that question is that " Flora, the lovely Roman," and Archipiada never were. Only one name of the three has come unscathed through the darkness of ignorance; the other two are fragmentary echoes of a forgotten past. There was nothing for Villon but the present, and the shadow of the Church and the Church's damnation over all. No doubt the sun shone then, and the trees burst into bud in the spring, and the corn ripened in the fields, and women were fair, and man's senses free to enjoy them; but the ambit of the human soul was circumscribed. It glanced backward into a darkness and forward into a terror. It was afraid.

The Renaissance meant for a moment the end of fear. The individual could stand alone once more, after more than a thousand years. And one of the first-fruits of his standing alone was the discovery that he was alone indeed. Galileo built his telescope and found that the earth moved round the sun. That was the great symbolic discovery of the Renaissance. And Shakespeare's work is the reaction of a prophetic soul to the discovery. It does not matter in the least whether Shakespeare knew of it or not; for Galileo's discovery was only the outward, visible sign of an inward and spiritual event, an event which we can see working in Shakespeare's soul. Man was not the centre of the universe, and man stood alone to face his destiny. The burden of the modern consciousness had begun.

Now the foundation of the modern consciousness is this, that the individual man takes his stand apart and alone, without the support of any authority, and claims to pass judgment for himself upon the life of which he is a part. He asks: By what, for what, shall he live? Here he is, involved in a vast process, in which evil seems as paramount as good, in which the noblest courage and the basest cowardice find a common end in death; here

LITERATURE AND RELIGION

he is, caught into a senseless and unmeaning riot in which glimpses of truth and beauty are apparently vouchsafed solely in order that man should be aware of the falsehood and ugliness which triumph over them. And he rebels against the sum of things. The modern consciousness is primarily a consciousness of rebellion; it begins with the demand that life should satisfy the individual's sense of justice and harmony.

And the old answer of orthodox Christianity, that the injustice and the pain of this life would be redeemed in a life to come, could satisfy no more. Men had come to feel that this life was a certainty and the future life a surmise which they had suffered to grow into a terror, frightening them from their true fulfilment on earth. The modern consciousness begins historically with the repudiation of established Christianity; it begins with the moment when men found in themselves the courage to doubt the life to come, and to free themselves from its menace in order to live this life more fully. It was necessary that man should come to his full stature, and that could only be done, as always, by his standing alone and assuming full responsibility for himself. What he *knew* to be true, that alone was true.

"What I know to be true; that alone is true." This has been the blazon on the banner of the Western consciousness since the Renaissance It seems a simple statement, just a straightforward challenge to external spiritual authority. And yet, in fact, that simple statement includes within it all the potentialities of the human soul. The whole of the human mystery is contained in the words "I know," just as it is contained in the words "I am." For what am I? And what is it that I know? The various answers to those ultimate questions

THE NECESSITY OF ART

mark the phases of the modern consciousness. But these phases are spiritual and transcendental; they are not neatly chronological. Though we can say truly that from the Renaissance to the present day the large and general movement has been towards seeking an ever deeper answer, it is equally true to say and equally important to recognize that there have been minds prophetic of the future. Not until Tolstoy and Dostoyevsky does another mind of Shakespeare's scope and comprehensiveness arise in European literature, and we find them following out the path marked out for them in Shakespeare's drama. Shakespeare had forefelt and foreknown their destiny; he had passed through the same discomfiture and arrived at the same necessity. All the literature which falls between those Titans of the modern consciousness is but a partial rediscovery of what Shakespeare already knew.

Unfortunately, I cannot permit myself at this moment to enter into that detailed examination of Shakespeare's work which is necessary in order to substantiate this assertion of mine. A whole book would barely be sufficient; a few pages of digression in an essay would be ludicrously inadequate. I must press on, instead, with the description of the evolution of the modern consciousness, unfolding under the sign: "What I know to be true, that alone is true."

There have been, there are eternally, two great types of answer to the question "What do I know?" There is the answer "I know the external world," and there is the answer "I know myself." At any moment in human history one or other of them is usually preponderant. For they correspond to two different *kinds* of knowledge. The knowledge of the external world is a knowledge

LITERATURE AND RELIGION

wherein the laws of cause and effect are operant; it is a rational knowledge of a realm of necessity, wherein the total conditions at a given moment are totally determined by the total conditions at the moment immediately before. There is no room for freedom in this world, and, in fact, no freedom is recognized. The knowledge of myself, on the other hand, or as we may call it for the sake of symmetry, the knowledge of the internal world, is a knowledge which is not governed by laws of cause and effect; it is an irrational, immediate knowledge, of a realm of freedom wherein the total conditions at a given moment are never totally determined by the total conditions at the moment before. There is no room for necessity in this world, and in fact no necessity is recognized.

Both these kinds of knowledge are knowledge. It is as impossible for me to deny that two and two make four, as it is for me to deny that I am free. But these kinds of knowledge are utterly different: one seems to come to me from without, the other to surge upward from within. And they are irreconcilable. The one, in pursuit of its own completeness, demands that the internal world should be of the same substance and subject to the same laws as the external world, that my integral and inviolable soul should be part of the realm of necessity, which seems absurd. The other, in pursuit of its completeness, demands that I should know the external world immediately as I know myself, which seems impossible.

This is the great paradox of the modern consciousness. It is, of course, much older than the Renaissance. It is universal in the world, and eternal in the human mind. But the awareness of the paradox has become most acute

THE NECESSITY OF ART

and reached an extreme of anxiety and indecision in the centuries since the Renaissance. For more than three hundred years—ever since the organized Christian Church ceased to be an unquestioned authority for the most gifted human minds—men have agonized over this paradox. The world has gone on; there has been famine and prosperity, and happiness and suffering, and wealth and poverty, just as there have always been. There has been colossal progress and colossal war, until now deep in our irrational souls we feel that we have reached a climacteric. The signs and tokens of madness and catastrophe multiply; and we begin to surmise that this paradox of the modern consciousness may be on the point of some slow solution.

But that is beyond my present scope. What is to be insisted upon here is, first, that the paradox is a religious problem—to be more accurate still, it is *the* religious problem, the only religious problem—and, secondly, that modern literature from the Renaissance until to-day has been pre-eminently occupied with it.

Now it is clear, from the very nature of the paradox, that no intellectual resolution is conceivable. The primary fact is man's consciousness of his own existence, his knowledge of himself as free: and that is an irrational knowledge. Whatever man does he must not deny this, simply because he will be forced to deny his own denial. He cannot really mechanize himself: if he attempts to, he merely deceives himself. The attempt to find a resolution from the side of the external world, *sub specie necessitatis*, is doomed to failure. So the resolution must be sought from the side of the internal world, *sub specie libertatis*. In other words man is inevitably driven to seek a non-rational comprehension of the world. He

LITERATURE AND RELIGION

cannot help himself: he must find a harmony: he cannot *live* in rebellion: he must reintegrate himself into life. So we find him cleaving, in literature, to the evidence of those moments of profound apprehension

> "When all the burden and the mystery
> Is lightened and . . .
> We see into the life of things."

The validity of such moments of apprehension is for the apprehender unquestioned: the quality of vision, to him who experiences it, is indubitable. For that moment he knows the world, even as he knows himself.

We may, if we like, call this moment of apprehension mystical. The name does not matter. Those who feel they can dismiss a knowledge when they have labelled it " mystical," may be freely permitted to smile their dismissal. It does not matter, indeed, whether we call it mystical, provided only that if we do, we remember that our immediate knowledge of our own self-existence is not a bit less " mystical " than this. These perceptions are of the same order; and it may even be that in the last analysis, one is not more intermittent than the other. The point of present importance, however, is that this " mystical " resolution of the paradox is what really distinguishes the Romantic movement in modern literature. On this Rousseau staked his all; this was at the creative centre of Wordsworth, of Shelley, of Keats and of Coleridge. The truest and deepest knowledge they found in themselves was in a moment of immediate apprehension of the unity of the world. They saw, or felt that they saw, that the great external world was not subject to the law of necessity—or rather not to the rational law of necessity; it was a living thing, an organism, which they knew as they knew the life within them. And it may seem strange that their apprehension of it should have been, in some sort, also an apprehension of necessity: of the necessity that what they saw must be thus and not otherwise. But this will seem strange only because we are hypnotized by words, and find it hard to realize that there is not one necessity, but two necessities, just as there is not one knowledge, but two knowledges. There is the necessity of the inanimate world conceived by the intellect, which is the necessary dependence of effect upon cause; and there is the necessity of the living organism, apprehended immediately, a compulsion to follow its own inward law of life. The "mystical" vision is a vision of *organic* necessity.

Such is the resolution of the great paradox sought by what is called the Romantic movement. It needs no saying that it is a deeply religious answer to a deeply religious problem. In any one of the true Romantics you may find at any moment a formulation of this perception of organic necessity as a perception of God; and I for my own part am convinced that if it is not a vision of God, it is assuredly a premonition of the divine. Here, for instance, is Robert Burns's statement:—

> "We know nothing, or next to nothing, of the structure of our souls, so we cannot account for those seeming caprices in them, that one should be particularly pleased with this thing, or struck with that, which, on minds of a different cast, makes no extraordinary impression. I have some favourite flowers in spring, among which are the mountain-daisy, the harebell, the foxglove, the wild-brier rose, the budding birch, and the hoary hawthorn, that I view and hang over with particular delight. I never hear the loud solitary whistle of the curlew in a summer noon, or the wild mixing cadence of a troop of gray plover in an autumnal

LITERATURE AND RELIGION

morning, without feeling an elevation of soul like the enthusiasm of devotion or poetry. Tell me, my dear friend, to what can this be owing ? Are we a piece of machinery, which, like the Æolian harp, passive, takes the impression of the passing accident; or do these workings argue something within us above the trodden clod ? I own myself partial to such proofs of those awful and important realities: a God that made all things, man's immaterial and immortal nature, and a world of weal or woe beyond the grave."

I choose that from Burns rather than the more famous passage from Keats, because it is so easily and so often assumed that the marvellous singer was really " the ignorant ploughboy " of legend and outside the charmed circle of our Romantic poets. He was of them, equal among equals.

But the peril of such perceptions is that they are momentary: they do not endure. Man may build a belief upon moments; yet he cannot live by them. The greater Romantics knew this also. Not a single one of those whom our literary history is accustomed to call our Romantics—except perhaps the Keats of the revised *Hyperion*—belonged to this higher order. And we shall never understand the real nature, or the deep significance, of Romanticism, until we understand that the whole of the epoch which we have called the modern consciousness is Romantic. The brief period which usually goes by that name is only a little segment of a great curve—a Romanticism within a Romanticism, as it were. Romanticism, essentially, is a movement of the soul which begins with the assertion of the I AM against all external spiritual authority, which proceeds from this condition of rebellion and isolation to a new life-adjustment, and goes on towards the ultimate recognition of a new principle of authority in and through the deeper knowledge of the self. Briefly, it may be called the rediscovery of the greater I AM through the lesser I AM. The phases of this great rhythmical motion are marked in the history of the human spirit from the Renaissance till to-day; but, as we have said, they are not wholly chronological. There were prophetic souls. At the beginning of the epoch stands Shakespeare, who comprehends within himself—" the prophetic soul of the wide world, Dreaming on things to come "—the whole movement of which lesser men were to manifest the phases after him. Shakespeare is a greater Romantic; so were Tolstoy and Dostoyevsky; so was, in some degree at least, Walt Whitman.

The distinctive quality of those whom I call the greater Romantics is that they should have completed within themselves the cycle of their being: in them the wheel has turned full circle. They have their moments of comprehension—one has only to read *The Phœnix and Turtle* to know how profound was the momentary understanding and acquiescence of Shakespeare—but the moment does not endure. Not that it ever loses its validity or its meaning; it remains as an earnest of the comprehension that may be, as a premonition of the harmony that is. But it is not enough; it is one-sided; implicit within it is a denial of life. Man cannot live by groping backward after old ecstasies. His knowledge must be steady and unwavering. It must not be intermittent; it must not be suprasensual; it must be a possession for ever. That is the crucial point. Man must *possess* his knowledge. It must not come to him as a visitant, and when it leaves him, leave him naked to the winds of reality. It is not a final, perhaps not even a human victory, that he should triumph for a moment

LITERATURE AND RELIGION

over the world of necessity and sink back to live in it as an alien and a sojourner. The reconciliation between the kingdom of necessity and the kingdom of freedom must not be subject to such vicissitude. In the last resort, it cannot be one-sided : or it will fail.

What distinguishes the greater Romantics is the recognition of the need of a solution of the paradox that is not one-sided. It is that humanity must find rest, not in a fleeting moment of heightened consciousness, but in a change of consciousness itself. A new beginning will be made, and a new generation born for which the paradox will not exist. The secular division between the intellectual consciousness (of necessity) and the intuitional consciousness (of freedom) will be no more. There will be a *known* harmony between the mysterious and as yet undiscovered reality which lies beneath the world of material phenomena and the reality of ourselves.

It is useless to try to describe this condition. A change, a fundamental change, in the human consciousness can only be dimly imagined and only symbolically expressed. Shakespeare's symbols are plain to read for those who can read symbols at all. There was a moment when all that he had done had no more interest for him ; when the writing of even the mightiest tragedies was for him a thing of no concern. The works of his latest period, which no one knows whether to call tragedies or comedies, works which are truly neither and for the most part are not in any intelligible sense works of art at all, have this meaning written plainly upon them. " I am weary, weary ; I am interested in one thing alone—to imagine the birth of a new generation for whom my struggles and torments and victories shall be only a dim,

THE NECESSITY OF ART

ancestral memory. The rest is for me only the idle weaving of words." And so, after playing half-wistfully with the figures of his imagination, in *The Winter's Tale*, in *Cymbeline*, in that part of *Pericles* that is indisputably his, after creating Perdita and Imogen and Marina, he gathered his strength together and conquered his own weariness to prophesy in *The Tempest*. The old consciousness fades away in Prospero : the greatest of all its inheritors resigns it to make way for the coming of a new consciousness in his loved child Miranda—

"O brave new world that has such people in it!"

I believe that *The Tempest* is the most perfect prophetic achievement of the Western mind. It is not Shakespeare's greatest work of art ; in one deep sense it is not a work of art at all, for the prime condition of its creation was that art in the ordinary meaning should have been relinquished and rejected. It is—if we are to call it art at all—the art that arises out of Shakespeare's deliberate abandonment of art. It belongs to the order of Tolstoy's later parables ; but it is still more profound than they are. It stands on the very verge of a condition that still lies far before the human soul. In Shakespeare the wheel had truly turned full circle, and because he was the prophet of what was to come, his last word is still latest. No Western mind has passed beyond *The Tempest;* none perhaps has gone so far.

> Shakespeare (says Novalis) was no calculator, no learned thinker; he was a mighty, many-gifted soul, whose feelings and works, like products of nature, bear the stamp of the same spirit; and in which the best and deepest of observers will still find new harmonies with the infinite structure of the universe; concurrences with later ideas, affinities with the

LITERATURE AND RELIGION

higher powers and senses of man. They are emblematic, have many meanings, are simple and inexhaustible, like products of nature; and nothing more unsuitable could be said of them than they are works of art, in that narrow mechanical acceptation of the word.

We are bound ever again and finally to return to Shakespeare in our pursuit of an understanding of the whole spiritual history of man since the Renaissance. Up to Shakespeare the spiritual history of man—I speak of the West alone—is comprehended within the Church; with him, it passes outside the Church. The severance was necessary and inevitable, for the sake of religion itself; simply because religion, if it is to be more than a comfortable and convenient narcotic, must be based on a challenge of the nature of things by the free spirit of man. And that again simply because man cannot *accept* certainties; he must discover them. An accepted certainty is not a certainty, a discovered certainty is. It is futile therefore for the priest to point to the final condition of a Shakespeare, a Tolstoy, or a Dostoyevsky, and say that he knew it all before. Is it not written in the Gospel: "Except ye be born again ye shall in nowise enter into the Kingdom of Heaven"? There, indeed, it is written. But how many people know what it means as these champions of humanity knew? No matter how beautifully, how profoundly, how finally Christ formulated the everlasting truths of religion, in order to know that they are everlasting, in order to know quite simply what they mean, man must rediscover them in himself.

The deepest-flowing tradition of Western literature is the process of challenge by the free human spirit ending in that rediscovery. If we can see that it is inevitable, it is only in so far as we can see that religion is a necessary

THE NECESSITY OF ART

motion of the human soul, a fundamental rhythm of man's being. Then it is plain that it must be fulfilled in literature, which is primarily an expression of that being. Then we can also recognize that there are greater and smaller fulfilments. In the master spirits the wheel truly turns full circle; in the lesser, it turns only half or quarter of the way. And, further, among these incomplete revolutions some may be conscious and others only instinctive. In those whom I have called the lesser Romantics—from Rousseau to Amiel—the fulfilments are conscious. The moment of vision and understanding is deliberately sought and directly acknowledged by these writers themselves, and it has been recognized by all men of religion who are not mere dogmatists as a central moment of religious experience. But we may go further than this, and declare that the originating experience of any truly creative work of literature, however small, is in some measure, and perhaps essentially, religious. That recognition by the writer of his theme, that delighted apprehension of his material, in the world outside him or within, seems to be nothing else than the sudden perception that an immaterial and all-pervading essence can be contained in a single symbol. What is perceived is perceived as something much greater than it is: as the philosophers put it, the universal is apprehended in and through the particular. This profound emotional recognition of the particular object or happening, as significant, as typical, as characteristic—an act of recognition which lies at the basis of all literary art and is as necessary to the simplest poem as it is recurrent in every considerable work of literature—seems to me fundamentally religious. There is a communication between mystery and mystery, between the unknown soul and the unknown

LITERATURE AND RELIGION

reality; at one particular point in the texture of life the hidden truth seems to break through the veil.

Dans certains états de l'âme presque surnaturels (wrote Baudelaire) la profondeur de la vie se revèle tout entière dans le spectacle, si ordinaire qu'il soit, qu'on a sous les yeux : il en devient le symbole.

Even this *âme damnée* had in his honesty to admit that the states of soul were " almost supernatural " ; and these supernatural states, which may be infinitesimal or overwhelming, these perceptions of a universal significance in the particular, are the primary stuff out of which literature is created.[1]

We have thus been working, as it were backwards, through a problem so vast and evasive that it might well be thought that a more orderly and logical presentment was indispensable. But, in sober truth, the subject is too vast for such a treatment in an essay. I have aimed at emphasizing those elements in it which seem to me to be even now but inadequately recognized. It is not worth while, in this place and with these necessary limitations, to insist upon a truth that is at the present time fairly generally, if half-heartedly admitted : namely, that there is an intimate connexion between both the creative perceptions that animate a work of literature and the responses those perceptions awaken in us, and the religious experience. But what seem to me the larger truths are not generally accepted. These, as I see them, are :

First, that religion is the deepest and most necessary motion of the free human soul ; as it were, a reflection in the consciousness of the inevitable adjustment to the

---

[1] For a more detailed exposition of this argument, the reader may be referred to the writer's *The Problem of Style*.

THE NECESSITY OF ART

primary law of life : and that it follows that literature, which is the most complete expression of the free human soul, *must* be religious, and that the greater the literature is, the more religious must, it be. This seems to me axiomatic : to one who has apprehended the full content of the word religion not even arguable. It can be recognized or not recognized : that is all.

Second, that religion, being of this fundamental kind, is by nature not to be confined in one medium of expression. At one time it may be an organized church which is the preponderant vehicle of the religious tradition. The continual process of rediscovery in the free human soul of the truth of religion may be accomplished at certain times mainly within a church, at others mainly without it. This will depend on whether the measure of freedom attainable by the soul is greater within a church than without, or greater without than within, at any given time. Where the freedom is greater, there will the stream of the vital religious tradition inevitably flow, because complete freedom is the necessary precondition of the religious rediscovery. Only through the fullest exploration of life can man *know* the laws of life.

Thirdly, the historical proposition that with the Renaissance the stream of religious tradition began to flow mainly outside the official Church. Science took upon itself the fulfilment of the outward exploration, literature the fulfilment of the inward exploration of life ; and literature, whose course was indicated in the prophetic mind of Shakespeare, assumed, sometimes consciously, sometimes unconsciously, the task of finding a mode of reconciliation between the realm of necessity and the realm of freedom. For the law of religious rediscovery is that man must apprehend the universe of his

LITERATURE AND RELIGION

fullest knowledge, within and without, as an *organic* unity.

Fourthly, that the conclusion reached by the literature which is most deeply expressive of the modern consciousness is that a fundamental change or rebirth of the human consciousness is necessary. Whether it is inevitable is another matter, outside the scope of this essay : I believe that it is.

Fifthly, that the whole great movement of the modern consciousness can be expressed completely for those who have experienced it within themselves, but only for those, in the sayings of Christ. As Shakespeare is prophetic of the last modern era of the Western consciousness, Christ was prophetic of the whole epoch, of which this last modern era is the culminating part.

Finally, that literature is become the great religious adventure of the human soul, simply because it affords the only complete expression to the adventuring human soul, and the human soul is bound upon an adventure which is necessarily religious. The meeting-ground of the lesser I AM with the greater I AM is still, after all the centuries, almost an unknown territory. *Hic Rhodus, hic salta.*

VII
THE DOCTRINE OF VALUES

VII

THE DOCTRINE OF VALUES

By Percy Dearmer

Art and the People

In old times there was no philosophy of æsthetic, because everybody was surrounded by beautiful objects and bad music did not (so far as we know) exist. There was no philosophy of æsthetic, just as there was no philosophy of beef or beer; people no more discussed the What and Why of art than they discussed (in those days) the What and Why of the atmosphere. It was only when they discovered that art was disappearing that they began to ask questions about it; and then the answer was ready. Had the questions been put before the sixteenth century, another answer would have been given, and it would have been a theological answer, partly because men were used to reasoning theologically and had not yet acquired a philosophy which ignored the Author of philosophy; partly because the Church had brought beauty up to the threshold of every peasant's cottage. In the days when the parish church was also the parish National Gallery, the parish Victoria and Albert Museum, and the parish Royal Academy of Music, there was no need to ask the Why of art. "We do it," would have been the answer, "to the glory of God," or even, as the Emperor Basil said when he ordered Vladimir's envoys to be taken to see the Liturgy in S. Sofia: "Let them see the glory of our

THE NECESSITY OF ART

God!" Obviously, since religion was equally for every man, and every man had a soul infinitely valuable in the sight of God, the art of the Church was for all, just as religion was for all.

But, unfortunately, no one thought of asking questions until art had long begun to disappear from the lives of the common people, and had become pedantic, and artificial, as a luxury of the rich. So when the answer was given to the question: "What is art, and Why?" the answer naturally was that art was an "extra," an embellishment of life which served to while away the time of the rich and to distinguish them from the less elegant rabble. Meanwhile great art had disappeared because it was not wanted. The age which first tried to answer the question: "What is art?" was the age of *rococo*, the age of *marqueterie*, the age when shepherds watched their flocks in porcelain.

The tradition survives. Suppose your town councillor or official is so highly intelligent and advanced a man that he decides to devote a quarter of an hour to discovering what actually art *is*, before he decides, for instance, that Croydon must be released of the incubus of the Whitgift Hospital, or that power-stations must be built at Holmbury Hill and Lulworth Cove. What better can he do than consult that palladium of our national intelligence, the *Encyclopædia Britannica?* That great work is, in fact, very seldom at fault; but, of course, the philosophy of art is just the weak point in its armour. The inquirer will find under the word "Æsthetics" much useful and true information; but he will also find it stated among other things that:—

1. "Æsthetic experience (in all but its simple and cruder forms) has been, and still is, *confined to a small number of*

THE DOCTRINE OF VALUES

persons; so that the subject does not appeal to a wide, popular interest."

2. "Both play and æsthetic contemplation . . . . contrast with the serious work imposed on us, and controlled by what we mark off as the necessities of life, such as providing for bodily wants, or rearing a family. They each add *a sort of luxurious fringe to life.*"

This was indeed the view of the nineteenth century, as it had been the view of the centuries immediately preceding. But it is not true.

1. So far from æsthetic experience being confined to the few, man in his long history has cared so much for beauty that he has put it before material comfort, and spent his time in making beautiful things when he often lacked bare necessaries of bodily life. The Chinese proverb: " If you have two loaves, sell one, and buy a lily," sums up the actual philosophy of man through countless centuries. Indeed the idea that æsthetic experience is something abnormal, " high-browed," or (as many of our barbarians still think) peculiarly feminine, is not true even of our people to-day, who have hardly emerged from the hideous commercialist materialism which triumphed in the Victorian era. The poor will pay more rent (as Charles Booth pointed out thirty years ago) for a house in a slum that has a creeper growing on it than for its uglier neighbours; all the hideous respectable houses of the 'sixties and 'seventies are being deserted by the well-to-do, and their rents fall year by year, because people will pay a great deal more for one of the pretty modern houses which architects now produce. Pictures, it is true, have a smaller circle of appreciators, but the idea that *art* is *pictures* is precisely the worst fallacy of the modern era; pictures require a highly trained judgment and are most difficult to understand—and yet,

THE NECESSITY OF ART

though they may make a naïve selection of favourites, the people do like pictures; and that they prefer canvases like Frith's " Derby Day " shows how genuine and healthy their appreciation is; for Frith's pictures are excellent work, and just what people ought to like before they have embarked in connoisseurship.

And all the people like dancing; and nearly all—even if they have no " ear "—like music. What is indeed more popular than singing, and dancing, and music streaming down the street? And how many recruits, I wonder, would join the Army if there were no bands and no dressing up? " Smart uniform " is printed on the recruiting placards, side by side with " healthy food." Of course the standard of taste varies in different classes. When people have a lesser quantity of (*a*) natural gifts, (*b*) disinterestedness, (*c*) general education, (*d*) special training, they naturally like inferior works of art; and if they are vulgar, their preferences are vulgar, too, of course. *But this does not mean that they are inartistic.* A person who prefers lighting a candle before a plaster cast of S. Anthony of Padua to attending the great services of the Church or studying the Gospels, is not irreligious : he is only inferior in his religion. And so it is with a person who prefers the lower and cheaper forms of art. . . . Yes, they *are* cheaper : and the poor man generally cannot afford good art. That is just the tacit conspiracy against him of which we complain—the unconscious or half-conscious conspiracy which nearly succeeded in closing the British Museum to him not long ago, which still barricades the National Gallery against him during the greater part of the week.

2. The second quotation from the *Encyclopædia* might be more shortly dealt with. *It simply is not*

THE DOCTRINE OF VALUES

true that æsthetic experience is a sort of luxurious fringe to life.

Æsthetic experience is one of the first necessaries of the spiritual life—of all life, that is, which is not a merely animal existence.

Art a Necessary

Art is a necessary of life, for the common people as for everyone else. It is not a luxury for the rich or a pastime for the leisured, or a frill tacked on to the real business of life. The mere vulgar materialist thinks it is; and if he happens to grow rich, he comes to regard art as important indeed, but important only as a means of ostentation.

But the mere vulgar materialist, be he rich or poor, thinks in the same way of religion: it is an extra. And if he becomes rich and patronizes it, he soon makes religion also into a means of ostentation. He litters our churches with tablets of what he has done To the Glory of his God, And in Memory of Sir Giorgius Midas, K.B.E.

If we had behind us two or three generations of sheer irreligion, people would think in the same way about religion as they do about art. We might still feel it necessary for our own personal lives, we might still feel its high value, but we should find it difficult not to drift into the habit of regarding it as something rather exceptional, and unnecessary to the common life of common men. Indeed, since the eighteenth century there has been a fairly widespread tendency so to regard religion. Against it the Church has protested in all her activities, making great sacrifices, devoting many lives—and often without much apparent result — because she believes passionately that life without religion is not worth living, that a materialist world would be a hell.

Why? Fundamentally because she believes—and all human experience is behind her—that life is not the mere satisfaction of material wants and the enjoyment of material pleasures, but that man is placed in a material environment in order that he may escape from it. A paradox! But it is the paradox of God. "Thou hast made us for thyself, and restless is our heart until it finds its rest in thee."

It is the same with art, and that is why art is so bound up with religion. Art also is a means of escape—a means of escape by different means, but to the same place—the Kingdom of Heaven. Historically, art and religion are bound up so close together that in the earlier records they cannot be distinguished one from another: both religion and art were regarded by man as so necessary that he willingly forwent his immediate needs in order to provide them—he would sleep under leaves in order to build a temple. At first they were combined in magic, which was the attempt of primitive man to obtain his desires by manipulating the unseen powers. The remarkable carvings and paintings by palæolithic men, which have been discovered in the caves of Altamira and elsewhere, were at first regarded as due to the craving for art; they are now recognized as magical in their origin—palæolithic man made them primarily because he thought he could thus influence the unseen powers to make the stags, mammoths, and fishes which he represented, breed more prolifically, and come more readily to his lure. His religion was egoistic and material (and we have never quite shaken off the " old man "); it was based upon the false analogy that, by making the image of something, you

THE DOCTRINE OF VALUES

could obtain control over the thing itself. It was, in fact, magic; but, so far as it went, it was a step in the right direction, the lowest rung in the ladder of escape.

And primitive man must have found that his skill in representation gave him a strange feeling of happiness. As a matter of fact these palæolithic paintings and carvings are amazingly good—they represent quite obviously a big step in the progress of civilization. The men who made them clearly loved the work, and the tribe must have loved looking at them. Something strange and new had come into life, a new emotion, a hint of a world that had no relation to the hunting of deer or the eating of raw mammoth. We call it art.

So another way of escape had been found by men, grovelling in the spiritual slime of primitive magic; and for long their art was a higher thing than their religion, leading it upwards towards the light.

We need not try to follow out the history. Just this one supremely interesting stage of evolution illustrates better than argument our two points—that art has been closely united to religion, and that both are means of escape from the sordid to the spiritual. Sometimes religion inspired art, sometimes a bad religion degraded art; sometimes art corrected a bad religion. Sometimes art has been itself degraded to a frivolous or sensual use; but this has happened almost wholly in that minute fragment of human history which has passed between the Humanist Movement and the present day. Before then it was the priests who were to blame! The artist did not invent idolatry: it was the people who wanted idols, and the priests who supplied them—" These be thy gods, O Israel!" A block of timber would suffice, as it does in India to-day. And when a sculptor was called in by the priests, he only did as he was told.

But he never did exactly as he was told. He could not help improving on his orders, and after a time he made the idols beautiful. Another way of escape had been found.

In Greece the images became beautiful: the gods were no longer terrifying monsters, they were human beings and easily passed into the fairy realm of mythology: thus it became possible for contemporary writers like Plato to speak of God almost as if they were Christians. The idol has become a harmless fancy, and the beauty which the sculptor had given it passes into the heavenly realm: for beauty is an attribute of the one true God, who made the heavens and the earth, and who made them in literal truth infinitely more beautiful than any human art.

The charlatan can lead men astray both in religion and in art, turning the one back to magic, melting the other down into luxury. But the saint and the artist both understand. They have had a vision; they have seen something of the Kingdom of Heaven; the veil has been lifted for a moment from before the glory of God. They cannot but respond: well or ill, they try to express what they have seen and felt: they cannot but proclaim what they know. And men follow them.

Christianity has made the secret more easy for men to understand: for it is the religion of incarnation, God expressing himself sacramentally to men. Therefore—in spite of the strain of morbid asceticism which has obscured the simple humanity of Christ's message during both mediæval and modern times—in the really catholic tradition of the Universal Church art has been accepted

THE DOCTRINE OF VALUES

and its principle understood. Material things are good and not bad, but their goodness lies in their not being regarded as ends in themselves; they are the medium of spiritual values; they are to be used sacramentally—that is to say, they are to be used as means of escape. Both art and sacramental religion recognize and love the material world, because it is the shadow of the Kingdom of Heaven, and they so use it as to bring men nearer to the God who made both heaven and earth. Sacramentalism makes this idea a part of the natural philosophy of the plain man.

I do not think then that the poor ever fell into the great modern heresy about art: it has always been an upper-class idea that art is only necessary to the rich, and a middle-class idea that art is not necessary to anybody. In the poor streets people will buy flowers even when they lack blankets, and every Sunday they put their little girls into white frocks, though they need the money and the time for more urgent things. They do not go to church very much, but they find little ways of escape. Sunday is different from other days: beauty struggles into the gloomy streets—pathetic little fragments of that glory of God which the streets shut out. They desire it; they want more of it. We might all help. In the poorest parish there is a church. It might in time become beautiful.

The Ultimate Values

Every man has a philosophy, even the man who cannot write his name. No one could get through a day without some working philosophy of life: and the important thing to find out about our friends and our enemies is

THE NECESSITY OF ART

what their philosophy is. But most people have no idea that they are actuated at every turn by so august a cause. They imagine that only a few clever men can be concerned with this high-sounding affair. And they probably think in their hearts that the clever men spend their lives in quite unpractical and futile speculations. Sometimes the clever men do. They really might help the plain man a little more—if they only said to him : " My dear friend, you have a philosophy ; and your philosophy, being based upon experience and much traditional wisdom, is probably a better one than mine ! " But they do not, and they disagree so much among themselves that people have an idea that there is no ultimate truth upon which the professional philosophers *are* agreed.

This is a mistake. They are agreed—or practically agreed—about several matters of the utmost importance. One of these is the matter of Values. The only novel thing about the doctrine of Values is that it has recently been more clearly marked out, more definitely proclaimed, and more practically recognized as a fundamental philosophy of life. To take one instance. Carlyle wrote in the middle of the last century that the great conviction of his life, the certainty that alone made him believe in God, was the reality of Truth, Goodness, and Righteousness. There you have a statement of the Ultimate Values. But it is not quite clear enough. He omits Beauty, and instead of it he makes a third Value by adding Righteousness, which is only another (and inferior) word for Goodness. He has the idea, the conviction, but he has not got it clearly analysed in his own mind.

Now what has helped the average plain man and has made him often more right than the metaphysician is that his philosophy has been a theology. It still is. He

THE DOCTRINE OF VALUES

believes, however vaguely, in the goodness of God, in eternal values, in immortality, in the pattern of Jesus Christ. This is the supreme value of a traditional theology. It supplies the plain man with a philosophy of life, which works, and which keeps him straight, in so far as he follows it.

The doctrine of Values is, then, not only agreed upon by the philosophers, but it is also ingrained in the plain man because of his Christian theology. Only it is not clearly defined or expressed in his mind. Let us therefore try to express it in a simple but condensed form, as it is generally understood to-day.

What is the philosophy behind what we have said in this book about the Necessity of Art, as it is behind Religion?

The philosophy behind all this is the most assured of all philosophies—that of the Absolute Values. Goodness is not the only quality which is absolute—above us, yet appealing within us, not made by us and yet shared in by us, an end in itself and therefore imperative. Truth and Beauty are also absolute and imperative; they also cannot be proved by anything else, but are each its own justification; they also are necessary to human life, in so far as it is good and distinguished from that of the animal world; they also demand disinterested homage, and yet bring the highest and most enduring happiness, enriching our personality in so far as we follow them.

There are only these three ultimate spiritual values—there is nothing else which is at once spiritual and good that cannot be included in these three categories. And there is no hierarchy among the Ultimate Values. Goodness is indeed more urgent than Beauty, and the absence of Truth more deplorable; but Beauty is more certainly manifested in Nature than Goodness, and has no problem of evil to reckon with; and whereas moral Goodness as we know it requires a struggle with evil, and in this form belongs to the world, Beauty is eternal, and we may say that it is already manifest as a heavenly thing—the beauty of Nature is indeed an earnest to us of the ultimate goodness that lies behind the apparent cruelty and moral confusion of organic life.

Yet we feel that these three are ultimately one, and human speech bears constant witness to the universal conviction that Goodness is beautiful, that Beauty is good, that Truth is Beauty. We can hardly avoid the use of the word "trinity," and if we are theists at all we cannot but say that they are one because they are the manifestation of one God. If we are not theists, there is no explanation.

Therefore the common man needs art as he needs religion; therefore the artist, in so far as he is a real artist and not a mere technical precisian, is religious. In so far as he is a real artist, he believes; in so far, he has found reality, he has found eternal life. In so far as he is a mere money-maker, imitator, parasite, or swaggerer, he has not found eternal life, and is not an artist. The artist may indeed care much for Beauty, and little for the other values; but in so far as he neglects Goodness and Truth, he is at least so much less of a man, and his art will be the worse for his insufficiencies. The moralist may also care little for other values; and, in so far as he does so, he also will be less of a man, and has often been a mere bleak Puritan, a Philistine, or a Pharisee, and sometimes an upright Inquisitor or a heartless prig. He may reach the Kingdom of Heaven with one eye

THE DOCTRINE OF VALUES

and one hand, but maimed he will always be. It is indeed necessary first of all that a man should be righteous, but the pious man who makes God's world hideous and depraved is only less bad than the impeccable partisan who shuns and distorts the truth.

A man may be a scientist or an artist with a less developed sense of the other values ; but half the weakness of science and art, half indeed, or more than half, of the world's unhappiness, is due to the narrow limitations in which we live. There is no need for these limitations to continue ; human beings ought to be released from them in their earliest education, and should be taught to be religious before they enter upon their work ; for religion is to believe in the Ultimate Values, and in the Unity behind them. A man who is properly religious may not equally understand them all, or have triple gifts ; but he will accept them all, reverence them all, and, in the measure of his capacity, will help them all to dominate the world.

www.ingramcontent.com/pod-product-compliance
Lightning Source LLC
Chambersburg PA
CBHW051929160426
43198CB00012B/2088